Far & Wide

With Paul Heiney and Joanna Pinnock

Where To Go and What To Do in East Anglia

ANGLIA
Television Limited

Foreword

Far & Wide presenters – Joanna Pinnock and Paul Heiney

Having lived in East Anglia for twenty years I thought I knew just about everywhere and everybody in it.

Yet, week after week *Far & Wide* has taken me into corners of this region I never knew existed, to meet people leading fascinating lives I had never heard of.

This is one of the greatest places in which to live and in which to produce a television programme like *Far & Wide*.

We have the finest landscapes of lowland Britain, a coastline of mystical beauty and a heritage of which true East Anglians have every right to be proud.

But, more importantly, we have the East Anglians themselves. They are a truly talented lot and every week has thrown up some new surprises as we captured working lives, traditional crafts being preserved, new skills being invented, places to visit, people to meet.

There's no shortage of any of them. The only problem is remembering them all for the next time your journey takes you into town, village, or countryside.

Which is why we've brought it all together in this book – so that the pleasure we hope you get from watching *Far & Wide* is with you as you travel around the region.

And to answer one question I am asked over and over again: "Are all those foods you taste really as good as they look?" I reply, "Yes! Oh, yes indeed."

Paul Heiney

* * * * *

I've always had a very special attachment to East Anglia. Every childhood holiday I can remember was spent in the region and it was then that I got completely hooked on the countryside. To a child from suburban London, the vast open skies, fields of red poppies and the song of the skylark were pure magic. All these years later, it's still my favourite part of the world.

Working on *Far & Wide* I've been able to explore new areas and re-visit favourite old haunts. But the one thing that's struck me is just how much more there is to discover in the region, no matter how well you think you know it. I've been to Cley many times, but never before gone in to the smokery, which is where Paul and I first met on a freezing December morning. We shook hands through the blue haze before sampling smoked mussels – not something I'd normally eat at nine in the morning but the smell was pretty appetizing. And they were very good!

Crab-fishing off Sheringham was a bit more of a challenge (my sea-legs never were very stable) and I don't think I will ever forget my bracing (?!) mid-Winter dip in the sea off Lowestoft. But if you don't fancy either of those, there are lots of other, less strenuous activities you can get involved in. You'll find some excellent footpaths and cycle routes in the region.

As for wildlife – well, East Anglia is well-known to be a birder's paradise. They flock here from all over the country and with settings as beautiful as the haunting Essex marshes and the dramatic crumbling cliffs of Dunwich, who can blame them? I'll certainly never forget the sight of the wild swans of Welney flying back on to the Ouse Washes, just as the sun was setting on a perfect late Winter evening.

I've had great fun exploring the region for *Far & Wide* and I hope this book will help you to do the same – whether you're discovering, or re-discovering, the magic of East Anglia.

Joanna Pinnock

Far & Wide

Contents

The Fens

Dominated by Ely Cathedral, Fenland is a low-lying region of Norfolk and Cambridgeshire with some of the richest farmland in Britain.

It was once effectively a boggy inland freshwater sea, with Ely standing as an island in the mud.

Drained 350 years ago – ironically on the orders of Cromwell, who had opposed the scheme when it was originally planned by King Charles I – the landscape has remained almost unchanged since.

But where once there was 3885 square kilometres (1500 square miles) of bog, less than 2.6 sq km (one square mile) remains now.

Botanist David Bellamy, who was evacuated to the area during the war, says of The Fens: "I have loved them ever since, not for the wetland wilderness they were but for what they are – a people-made landscape, as full to the brim with heritage as they are with water."

i Tourist Information Centres

Downham Market
Tel. 01366 387440
e-mail: downham-market@west-norfolk.gov.uk

Ely
Tel. 01353 662062; Fax. 01353 668518
e-mail: elyTIC@compuserve.com

Wisbech
Tel. 01945 583263; Fax. 01945 463078

Ordnance Survey Maps
OS Landranger sheet numbers: 142, 143

Ely Cathedral – 'The Ship of the Fens'

Downham Market

King Charles I was not a happy man when he visited Downham Market in 1645.

He had just been defeated at the battle of Naseby and is said to have stayed at a previous version of the High Street Swan Inn – disguised as a clergyman!

The village school also had famous visitors. Denver-born Captain George Manby, who invented a mortar which could fire life-saving lines from shore to shipwreck, was a pupil and Admiral Horatio Nelson, it is said, also spent time there.

Given that it is in an area so influenced by engineers from the Low Countries, it is hardly surprising that this attractive Ouse-side town displays so much Dutch influence in its buildings.

Downham dates back to Saxon times and had achieved market status by the mid-11th century – although what was originally a Saturday event is now held on Fridays and Saturdays.

Downham Market Area

Collector's World of Eric St John Foti

An eclectic range of objects – from cars to carts and books to bottles – brought together by an inveterate collector during his extensive travels in England and abroad.

Features include the only exclusively Armstrong Siddeley car collection open to the public and a Nelson Room which celebrates the life of this North West Norfolk-born and locally-educated hero and displays his birth and marriage certificates.

There is also a Pink Room, dedicated to prolific romantic authoress Barbara Cartland, a special children's section and another devoted to the sights and sounds of Dickensian England.

The collection – which has been featured on television – can be found

at Hermitage Hall, Downham and is open daily from 11am to 4pm with special Christmas events held from mid-December between 12.30pm and 4.30pm.

Denver Mill

The original mill at Denver – the village where Captain Manby was born – was built in 1835.

It continued grinding corn, using wind-power, for more than a hundred years before its sails were struck by lightning in 1941.

The newly restored structure is a fine example of a traditional working mill and a unique tour takes the visitor to every corner.

Not surprisingly, the teashop and bakery offer products made with the mill's own flour – and there is also a visitor centre, craft centre and holiday accommodation on site.

The mill is open daily all year round – between at least 10am and 4pm from Monday to Saturday and from at least 12 noon to 4pm on Sundays.

Denver Sluice

If sluices can be famous, then Denver Sluice is an absolute star – its gates capable of holding a tidal rise of nearly 7.5m (24ft) on the seaward side.

The sluice is responsible for a crucial area of drainage and can clear flood water from 325,000 hectares (800,000 acres) of fenland.

Ouse Washes

Winter is the best time to visit this bleak landscape, large chunks of which, because of its importance to birds, were bought up by the RSPB, Wildfowl and Wetlands Trust and Cambridgeshire Wildlife Trust or were left as legacies.

The Ouse Washes are just under a kilometre (half-mile) wide strip of

A typical Fenland scene viewed from Denver Sluice

☎   FAX   💻

Collector's World
Tel. 01366 383185
Fax. 01366 386519

Denver Mill
Tel./Fax. 01366 384009

Ouse Washes Reserve
Tel. 01354 680212

Wildfowl and Wetlands Trust Welney Reserve
Tel. 01353 860711
Fax. 01353 860711
e-mail: welney@wwt.org.uk
web: www.wwt.org.uk

permanent grassland lying between the parallel banks of the Old and New Bedford Rivers and run for 32 kilometres (20 miles) from Earith in the south west to Denver in the north east.

Their 2469 hectares (6100 acres) of washland make up one of the most important and biggest man-made freshwater grassland sites in Europe – protected under the Ramsar convention and listed as a Site of Special Scientific Interest.

The site, nearly 10 kilometres (six miles) east of Chatteris on the A142/A141 between Ely and March, floods in Winter and attracts thousands of Bewick's and Whooper swans.

The Wildfowl & Wetlands Trust, which runs the **Welney Centre reserve,** was founded by the late artist and naturalist Sir Peter Scott in 1946 at Slimbridge, Gloucestershire.

A highlight of the programme here is 'Wild Birds by Floodlight' – an evening spectacle organised from early November to the end of February (booking for groups is essential).

One of the WWT wardens gives a live commentary as he feeds thousands of wild birds.

In recent Winters, the Fenland reserves have attracted almost 5000 Bewicks and some 1500 Whoopers – to boast perhaps the largest concentration of swans in Europe.

Other birds seen at this time include grebes, cormorants, mute swan, geese, shelduck, gadwall, teal, mallard, pintail, tufted duck, marsh harrier, peregrine falcon, lapwing, ruff, gulls and wigeon.

The Ouse Washes represents probably the best site in Cambridgeshire for dragonflies – with species including the Variable Damselfly, Scarce Chaser and the Hairy Dragonfly to be seen.

The Wildfowl and Wetlands Trust at Welney is open daily from 10am to 5pm all year round (closed Christmas Day) and from mid-November until mid-March each year visitors can see the flocks being fed at 3.30pm daily.

Dogs, with the exception of guide dogs, are not allowed at Welney but are accepted on leads at the RSPB Ouse Washes.

Welney Nature Reserve

Ely

Despite being the second smallest city in England, Ely boasts some of the greatest names from its history.

In the 11th century, it represented the perfect refuge for Hereward the Wake – a semi-mythical figure, who led a stubborn resistance to the Norman invaders.

Another former resident was Oliver Cromwell and Ely is considered lucky – because it was spared the devastation he wrought elsewhere.

Today a large general market – which dates back to Monastic times but was switched from Saturdays to Thursdays in 1801 – attracts people from all over the district.

Special events held during the course of the year in Ely include a May fair and, in July, an 'Aquafest', folk weekend and – not least – the World Pea Shooting championships!

Ely Cathedral

Ely Cathedral (nicknamed 'The Ship of the Fens') rises above the landscape in spectacular fashion – its unique lantern tower providing a welcome sight for the lost or weary traveller.

The Cathedral, which dates back to 1081, was built on the site of an original double monastery founded by St Etheldreda, daughter of an Anglo-Saxon king, in 673.

Completed in 1189, it was designed as a fantastic structure to house her shrine, which attracted hundreds and thousands of pilgrims throughout the Middle Ages.

Undoubtedly the most famous feature of Ely Cathedral is the incredible octagonal lantern, a breathtaking and gravity-defying wooden structure begun when the original Norman tower

Oliver Cromwell's House, Ely

collapsed in 1322.

In the 17th century, at the time of the Civil War, Cromwell entered the Cathedral with soldiers during a service and shut it for some 17 years.

The Cathedral, which for many years has had strong links with Cambridge University, is open daily from at least 7.30am to 5pm throughout the year.

There are regular free guided tours and guides can be booked for visiting groups all year round.

Ely Museum

A fascinating museum that tells the history of the Isle of Ely and the Cathedral city from the Ice Age to modern days.

Sometimes actors play the part of prisoners in the cells and re-enact the visit of 18th century penal reformer John Howard.

The museum is open daily, including on Bank Holidays, between at least 10.30am and 4.30pm.

Ely River Cruises

Operated by Cambridge River Cruises from Ship Lane at weekends between April and September and daily from Wednesday to Sunday during holiday periods.

The 12-seater Edwardian-style launch used for the 30-minute tours of the Ely waterfront is also available for private hire at other times.

Monastic Buildings

The Cathedral is set within the walls of the Benedictine Monastery – and a walk round the college reveals evidence to back Ely's claim to the largest collection of medieval domestic architecture in England.

Oliver Cromwell's House

Now comprehensively restored, the former home of the Lord Protector hosts an imaginative recreation of 17th century life.

Period rooms, displays and videos tell the stories of the draining of the fens and of Cromwell, who moved to the city in 1636 after inheriting estates and property from his Stuntney-based uncle.

Cromwell also inherited the position of 'Farmer of the Tithes' of the two Ely parishes and was responsible for collecting money and goods in kind.

For children there is today a 'haunted bedroom' and a dressing up box with soldiers' hats to try on.

The building, open daily all year round, doubles as home to the local Tourist Information Centre, which can arrange various available tours, including the Ely Ghost Walk.

It also sells information packs about both circular walks in the area and Fen Rivers Way, which runs from Cambridge to King's Lynn via Ely.

Stained Glass Museum

Housed in the Cathedral, this unique museum – which is open all year – is dedicated to the rescue and display of stained glass.

Through the hundred panels on show, visitors can trace the history of this fascinating craft from the Middle Ages to the present day.

St Mary's Church

Although its proximity to the Cathedral means it is easy to overlook, St Mary's is worth a visit.

The 13th century church, built by Bishop Eustace, was the setting for the baptism of Cromwell's youngest daughter in 1638.

A feature of particular interest is a tablet, which is set in the tower wall and commemorates some of those who died in the Littleport riots – prompted by famine – in 1816.

The Old Fire Engine House

This 18th century building, close to St Mary's, once – as its name suggests – housed the local fire engine.

For at least the last 32 years, however, it has been a restaurant – with the water tender giving way to tender loving care in the preparation of food.

It is mentioned in the Good Food Guide as one of the longest-serving restaurants in the country and is widely known for its Fenland food and traditional British cuisine.

Ely Area

Byways Water Garden

Water gardens with large ponds containing koi carp and supplying everything for the water gardening enthusiast.

Byways is open between 9.30am and 5.30pm all year round.

Chatteris

In its early days, this quiet country town is thought to have been the last refuge for Queen Boudicca and the Iceni people as they fled from massacre at the hands of the Romans.

Handsome houses and a few hostelries – the High Street's Cross Keys is an original coaching inn – survive from the 19th century, when there was a daily coach service to London.

The town's **museum,** in Church Lane (open on Saturdays, Sunday afternoons and Tuesday evenings) has local interest exhibits which include some 18th century mobile stocks and long bamboo poles used for collecting money from upstairs windows on Hospital Sunday.

Ely Cathedral
Tel. 01353 667735
web: www.cathedral.ely.
anglican.org

Ely Museum
Tel. 01353 666655
Fax. 01353 659259

**Ely River Cruises
(Talking timetable)**
Tel. 01223 300100

Oliver Cromwell's House
Tel. 01353 662062
Fax. 01353 668518

**Ely Cathedral Stained
Glass Museum**
Tel. 01353 660347
Fax. 01353 327367
e-mail: stainedg@
lineone.net

The Old Fire Engine House
Tel. 01353 662582
Fax. 01353 668364

Byways Water Garden
Tel. 01353 740798

Chatteris Museum
Tel. 01354 696319

Chatteris

Downfield Windmill

Constructed as a smock mill in 1726, Downfield – also known as Pollards Mill – was rebuilt as an eight-sided tower mill after the original was destroyed by gales in 1890.

Today it still grinds corn and produces a range of flour in wholemeal, brown and white grades, which can be purchased direct from the millers.

Downfield is open between 11am and 5pm on Sundays and Bank Holidays only.

Hadenham Windmill

Built in 1803 for Daniel Cockle, the Great Mill overlooking the fenland countryside has four sails and three sets of stones – one of which remains in use.

Restoration of the mill, which lies south west of Ely and last worked commercially in 1946, began in 1992 and was completed six years later.

It is now open on the first Sunday of each month and – by appointment only – between 2pm and 6pm from May to September.

Littleport Show

The whole of the small village of Littleport, just north of Ely, rallies to play a part in this July show, held on fields close to the town centre.

Visitors travel from all over East Anglia to the community event, which features heavy horse displays, show jumping competitions and various other activities and attractions.

Stretham Old Engine

Mepal Outdoor Centre

Located on the A142 between Sutton and Chatteris, Mepal is a family outdoor leisure centre with facilities including a campsite, children's play park, a three-zone paintball site, boat hire and café.

Northfield Windmill

Known also as Townsend or The Shade Windmill, this former drainage mill – at the north end of Soham – is one of the smallest in Cambridgeshire.

It once occupied another site but was converted and moved to its present location in 1830.

Prickwillow Drainage Museum

This small village takes it name from the 'prickets', or skewers, of willow which the hardy local inhabitants, known as 'Fen Tigers', would cut to hold down thatch.

Its museum was set up in 1982 by a band of enthusiasts whose aim was to save, restore and preserve the old engines from Prickwillow and various other pumping stations, where they worked to keep the surrounding fenland drained.

Extensions and improvements to the original building have provided a viewing gallery, tea room and souvenir shop.

The museum is open daily between 11am and 5pm from the beginning of May to the end of September and between 11am and 4pm at week-ends only from the beginning of March to the end of April and the beginning of October to the end of November.

Special 'run days' are usually held once a month from May to December (phone for details).

RAF Witchford Display

A small exhibition of memorabilia from the local RAF station which operated between 1943 and 1946 along with some memorabilia from RAF Mepal.

The display, at Lancaster Business Park, Witchford – just to the

Northfield Windmill

south-east of Ely – is open between 10am and 4.30pm Monday to Friday and on Sundays (except Bank Holidays) from May to September.

Soham

Now the second largest settlement in East Cambridgeshire, Soham was a tiny encampment beside a mere (inland waterway) before the fens were drained.

Although a Saxon Cathedral east of the present main street was destroyed in the Viking raids of 870 AD, Soham retains a firm association with its founder, St Felix of Burgundy.

Over the centuries, the town has spread from its original heart and these days the busy A142 diverts traffic around the town, where a weekly market is held on Fridays.

Stretham Old Engine

This restored brick engine house contains an 1831 land drainage engine, once driven by steam and responsible for draining about 1619 hectares (4000 acres) of land.

On advertised dates the engine and its wooden scoop wheel – the last surviving complete examples of their kind in the Fens – are rotated by an electrical drive to show how they originally worked.

Streatham Old Engine is open to visitors between 11.30am and 5pm on Sundays and Bank Holidays only from Easter to the end of September – but can open at other times for school parties.

Wicken Fen

See South Cambridgeshire chapter (Page 26).

Wisbech

The 'Capital of the Fens' grew up around its trading port and began to flourish with the drainage of the Fens in the 17th century.

Tremendous growth took place in the 17th and 18th centuries, resulting in the fine buildings which today give Wisbech the air of a prosperous Georgian town.

Despite the decline of the port, Wisbech is still the market centre for agricultural and horticultural produce from much of the surrounding area.

Some areas of the town may strike a chord with visitors who saw the television adaptation of Charles Dickens' 'David Copperfield' – as Wisbech was used as one of the locations for the series, starring Bob Hoskins, Nicholas Lyndhurst, Pauline Quirke and Maggie Smith.

Angles Theatre & Arts Centre

The Angles is one of the oldest working theatres in the country and is, in many ways, unique.

It has its own in-house amateur company and also offers an extensive programme of entertainment ranging from concerts to dance and drama, exhibitions, talent competitions, talks and workshops.

Elgoods Brewery and Gardens

Real ales have been brewed on this North Brink site for over 200 years and the Elgood family has been continuing the process for the past 120 or so.

As well as the classic Georgian brewery, the site today includes a restored 1.6 hectare (four-acre) garden, a gift and plant shop and a café and licensed bar.

Guided brewery tours and tastings are held at 2pm on Wednesdays, Thursdays and Fridays from the beginning of May to the end of September and the garden is open to visitors between 1pm and 5pm from Wednesday to Sunday as well as on Bank Holiday Mondays.

Elgoods Brewery and Gardens, Wisbech

Lilian Ream Photographic Gallery

Housed in the Bridge Street Tourist Information Centre, this gallery contains a display of historic photographs by an enterprising woman photographer from Wisbech at the end of the last century.

By the time she died at the age of 84 in 1961, Lilian Ream had amassed a collection of more than 100,000 images of people, places and events, providing a fascinating insight into life in the town.

The gallery is open between 9.30am and 5pm from Monday to Saturday all year round.

Octavia Hill Birthplace Museum

This Georgian Grade II* listed building on the South Brink at Wisbech is where the co-founder of the National Trust was born.

It opened as a museum in 1995

Octavia Hill Birthplace Museum, Wisbech

Downfield Windmill
Tel. 01353 720333

Hadenham Windmill
Tel. 01353 740798

Mepal Outdoor Centre
Tel. 01353 692251

Prickwillow Drainage Engine Museum
Tel. 01353 688360
organiser
Tel. 01353 688230

RAF Witchford Display
Tel. 01353 666666 or 664934

Stretham Old Engine (Curator)
Tel. 01353 649210

Angles Theatre
administration
Tel. 01945 585587
bookings
Tel. 01945 474447
e-mail: angles@ userone.co.uk

Elgoods Brewery and Garden
Tel. 01945 583160
Fax. 01945 587711

Lilian Ream Photographic Gallery
Tel. 01945 583263

Octavia Hill Birthplace Museum
Tel. 01945 476358

Peckover House, Wisbech

and records the life and work of Octavia, her family and fellow workers for housing reform.

As part of her housing work, Octavia encouraged the creation of small open spaces to bring 'the healthy gift of air and joy of plants and flowers' to grim urban conditions.

Her vigorous public campaigns to save recreational open space accessible to all, led to the creation of the National Trust in 1895.

The South Brink museum is open between 2pm and 5.30pm on Wednesdays, Saturdays, Sundays and Bank Holiday Mondays from March to the end of October (and at other times by appointment).

Peckover House

On the North Brink of the River Nene in Wisbech, there's one of the most elegant terraces of Georgian town houses in the country.

But there's one house, and particularly its garden, which is worth more detailed investigation – and not only because it played the part of Mrs Steerforth's house in 'David Copperfield'.

Peckover House was given to the National Trust in 1948 after being in the hands of a local Quaker banking family for more than 170 years.

One wing was originally used as a bank by the townspeople but today it's the 0.8 hectare (two-acre garden) that the majority of visitors come to see – mostly because it's so unusual to find such a splendid Victorian garden behind a Georgian house.

It results from the acquisition by the Peckover family of several other gardens along the North Brink throughout the 19th century, so that they could extend their own.

Today it's crammed with plants, topiary and magnificent trees, including some 300-year-old orange trees – a veritable feast for the eyes of a garden lover.

Towering above in one part of the garden is a magnificent Chusan palm, alongside a splendid South American Monkey Puzzle Tree while a Maidenhair tree was one of the tallest in the country until it was struck by lightning in 1977 and the top broke off.

Many of the trees in the orangery date back to the 1600s – and still bear fruit – while the fernery houses a wonderful mixture of specimens, many of them unusual.

The gardens never stop developing but Peckover remains an outstanding example of the Victorian Gardenesque style, in which the display of individual plants is as important as the overall effect.

The house and garden at Peckover are open between 12.30 and 5.30pm on Wednesdays, Saturdays, Sundays and Bank Holiday Mondays from the beginning of April to the end of October.

The gardens alone are also open between the same dates and times on Mondays, Tuesdays and Thursdays.

There are refreshments, toilets and some disabled facilities on site.

Thomas Clarkson Memorial

This impressive memorial to a son of Wisbech who – pressing for the ending of the African slave trade – was one of the earliest leaders of the Abolitionist Movement, towers over Bridge Street.

Wisbech & Fenland Museum

Located close to St Peter's Church and the fine Georgian Crescent, this is one of the oldest purpose-built museums in the country – dating back to the creation of a Museum Society in 1835.

The current building, constructed in 1847, was originally shared with the Literary Society and still retains its large library.

Collections extend across a broad range of subjects, including local history and archaeology, archives, art, natural history and photography.

The museum library – which contains some 12,000 volumes, mostly from the 19th century – is open to the public on the first Saturday of each month with a programme of temporary exhibitions.

Perhaps the most interesting item – and one which is on permanent display – is the original manuscript for Charles Dickens' Great Expectations.

The main museum is open from Tuesday to Saturday only (excluding Bank Holidays) between 10am and 5pm from April to September and between 10am and 4pm from October to March.

Wisbech Castle

Although not open to the public, this interesting building – which looks like, and is, a small decorous Georgian villa – can be seen from Castle Yard and The Crescent.

The present building stands on the site of the original Norman

Thomas Clarkson Memorial, Wisbech

Fenland & West Norfolk Aviation Museum

castle, which was founded by William I in 1072 and, although passed to the Bishops of Ely at an early date, remained a significant location for the royals.

Completely rebuilt in the late 15th century, the now extinct castle is said to have been visited several times by Edward I – and King John, who was bound for Wisbech when he lost his crown in The Wash.

The present 'castle' – which replaced a mansion for Oliver Cromwell's Secretary of State – was constructed by local builder and developer Joseph Medworth, responsible also for the crescents north and south of the grounds, in 1816.

TV addicts may be interested to know The Castle doubled as Mr Wickfield's home in the small screen version of 'David Copperfield'.

Wisbech Area

Dunhams Wood

Margaret and Arthur Dunham planted this 1.6 hectare (four-acre) site with a great variety of unusual trees – rare in themselves in the Fens.

Interspersed among them are various sculptures and a small-gauge miniature railway.

The site, at Rodham Road, March, is open between 2 and 5pm on Bank Holiday Sundays and Mondays from Easter to August as well as the last Sunday in July and every Sunday in August.

Fenland & West Norfolk Aviation Museum

The museum claims one of the finest and most interesting collections of

aviation archaeology in the country.

Many of the exhibits relate to the Second World War but there is also memorabilia taking in both earlier and later periods – including the Falklands conflict and the Gulf war.

An English Electric Lightning, Hunting Jet Provost T3 and De Havilland Vampire T11 are on display outside and access to the cockpit of all three aircraft is available every day the museum is open, subject to staffing and weather conditions.

Inside visitors can sample the 'hot seat' in a 747 Jumbo jet cockpit simulator and, on certain days (please inquire), a Jet Provost systems trainer.

The museum, which features a gift shop, is situated at Bamber's Garden Centre, on the B198 (Old Lynn Road) at West Walton – approximately 0.8 kilometres (half a mile) off the A47 Wisbech bypass.

It is open at weekends and on Bank Holidays only between 9.30am and 5pm from April to September and 10am and 4pm in March and October.

March

A pleasant and relaxing market town, which was once an island surrounded by marshes.

The River Nene winds its way through the town and moorings in the centre are close to shops, the riverside park and leisure centre.

March museum, in the High Street (open on Wednesday mornings, Saturdays and some Sundays throughout the year), features exhibits including a reconstructed Fenland cottage and a privy.

Elsewhere, St Wendreda's Church (key available from Stars public house) was said by Sir John Betjeman to be "worth cycling 40 miles in a head wind to see."

On the outskirts of the town is Stonea Camp (open at all times), built as the lowest 'hill fort' in Britain and used, unsuccessfully, against the Romans.

Its banks and ditches were restored in 1991 following archaeological excavations.

Peckover House
Tel./Fax. 01945 583463

Wisbech & Fenland Museum
Tel. 01945 583817

Dunhams Wood
Tel. 01354 652134

Fenland & West Norfolk Aviation Museum
Tel. 01945 584440

March Museum
Tel. 01354 655300

Parson Drove Visitor Centre

Known as 'The Cage', this is a Victorian lock-up in a village green setting, near the Swan inn at Parson Drove, just over nine kilometres (six miles) west of Wisbech.

The building has an interesting 170-year history and contains a documented and photographic record of a fenland village.

The Visitor Centre is open from the beginning of April to mid-October between 2 and 5pm on Wednesdays as well as between 1 and 5pm on Saturdays, Sundays and Bank Holidays.

March town centre

West Cambridgeshire

An area full of fascinating market towns with interesting histories, along with ancient abbeys and the cathedral city of Peterborough.

In the Nene Valley there are charming stone villages, along the Ouse Valley tranquil riverside settlements and, in the west of the district, some magnificent church spires.

Famous associated historical figures include Oliver Cromwell, diarist Samuel Pepys, poet William Cowper and Catherine of Aragon.

More recently Huntingdon alone has boasted links with gardener Capability Brown, Rolls Royce co-founder Henry Royce, the writer Dorothy L. Sayers and former Prime Minister John Major.

i Tourist Information Centres

Huntingdon
Tel. 01480 388588; Fax. 01480 388591
e-mail: adele.dant@huntsdc.gov.uk

Peterborough
Tel. 01733 452336; Fax. 01733 452353

Stamford
Tel./Fax. 01780755611
e-mail: tourism@skdc.com

St. Neots
Tel. 01480 388788; Fax. 01480 388791
e-mail: adele.dant@huntsdc.gov.uk

Ordnance Survey Maps
OS Landranger sheet numbers: 141, 142

The River Welland, Stamford

Peterborough

The colourful past of this city extends from prehistoric times to occupation by the Romans, the arrival of the Saxons and, more recently, the burial of two Tudor queens.

It has links with the poet and author John Clare, Nurse Edith Cavell (also strongly connected with Norwich) and Hereward the Wake.

Peterborough's museum now holds one of the largest collections of Clare material in the world (the other being at Northampton Central Library).

The modern city still retains evidence of the engineering businesses which arrived as the industrial revolution took shape and is something of a shopper's delight with complexes such as the Hereward Cross, Queensgate, Rivergate and Serpentine centres.

Brewery Tap

Peterborough's first working brewery for 70 years can be visited at Westgate by arrangement.

The brew-pub serves award-winning Oakham ales and a selection of guest beers.

Cathedral

Once a Benedictine Abbey, the Cathedral was created by Henry VIII, whose first wife – Catherine of Aragon – is buried here.

The site was also, for a time, the resting-place of Mary Queen of Scots, following her execution at Fotheringay.

Catherine's tomb suffered badly at the hands of Cromwell's troops but Mary's escaped, thanks to her son – James VI of Scotland and I of England – who had his mother's remains transferred to Westminster Abbey.

Other Cathedral features which survived this time of Cromwell include the fan vaulting designed by John Wastell – who went on to build King's College chapel in Cambridge – and, in the nave, the largest surviving Medieval painted ceiling in Europe.

The Cathedral is open to visitors throughout the year between 8.30am and 5.15pm from Monday to Saturday and between 12 noon and 5.15pm on Sundays.

Key Ferry Cruises

Operating from the city's Embankment, next to the Key Theatre, the cruises run from April to October and last between one and four hours.

Key Theatre

Situated in attractive surroundings close to the city centre and on the bank of the River Nene, this charming and intimate theatre offers a wide range of entertainment.

Longthorpe Tower

Northern Europe's finest complete set of domestic wall paintings of the time can be found in this 14th century tower of a fortified manor house.

The tower is open between 12 noon and 5pm over weekends and Bank Holidays from the beginning of April to the end of October.

Museum and Art Gallery

The museum, with exhibits covering archaeology, geology and local history, is open between 10am and 5pm from Tuesday to Saturday throughout the year.

Railworld

A small railway museum open daily between 11am and 4pm – except from November to February when visitors are admitted Monday to Friday only.

Displays – which include an impressive model railway – cover various rail topics and there are exhibits about past and present train travel, world-wide.

The Cresset

Peterborough's biggest leisure and entertainment complex features a café and coffee shop, dance studio, indoor shopping, a library, pub, soft play centre and squash courts.

Peterborough Cathedral

It is also the venue for concerts, comedy nights and regular collectors' fairs and markets.

Thorpe Hall

Built during the reign of Cromwell, the hall – at Longthorpe, Peterborough – now houses a Sue Ryder palliative care home.

However, the ground floor can be visited by appointment and the gardens are open all year round, except at Christmas and New Year.

☎ FAX 🖥

Brewery Tap
Tel. 01733 358500

Peterborough Cathedral
Tel. 01733 343342

Key ferry cruises
Tel. 01933 680743

Key Theatre
(Box office)
Tel. 01733 552439

Longthorpe Tower
Tel. 01733 268482

Peterborough Museum & Art Gallery
Tel. 01733 343320
Fax. 01733 341928

Railworld
Tel. 01733 344240

The Cresset
Tel. 01733 265705

Thorpe Hall
Tel. 01733 333922

Crowland or Croyland Abbey

The Abbey – on the A1073, 13 kilometres (eight miles) north of Peterborough – was founded as a hermitage by a Saxon saint and became one of the most important Benedictine monasteries in the land.

Crowland is open daily from dawn to dusk throughout the year.

East of England Showground

The home of the annual agricultural show also acts as host to the regular Truck-Fest, Peterborough's speedway team and a number of other events held in the middle of the week and on most Friday evenings.

The site, which also boasts a golf driving range and pitch and putt course, is open daily.

Crowland Abbey
Tel. 01733 210499

East of England Showground
Tel. 01733 234451

Elton Hall
Tel. 01832 280468
Fax. 01832 280584

Flag Fen
Tel. 01733 313414
Fax. 01733 349957
web: www.flagfen.
freeserve.co.uk

National Dragonfly Museum
Tel. 01832 272427

Nene Country Park
Tel. 01733 234443

Ferry Meadows Watersports Centre
Tel. 01733 234418

Orton Meadows Golf Course and Pitch and Putt
Tel. 01733 237478

Nene Valley Railway
Tel. 01780 784444
Fax. 01780 784440
web: www.internetlink.
co.uk/nvr.htm

Crowland or Croyland Abbey

Elton Hall

The home of the Proby family, which is open on specific days from May to August, is full of works of art and treasures spanning the hall's 500-year existence.

These include fine furniture, a library with 12,000 books – including the prayer book of Henry VIII – and outstanding paintings by such artists as Constable, Gainsborough and Reynolds.

The mixed grounds – open between 2 and 5pm on Wednesdays in June and additionally on Thursdays, Sundays and Bank Holiday Mondays in July and August – include a large rose garden, a herbaceous garden and a lily pond.

Flag Fen Bronze Age Excavations

This re-created fenland environment at Fourth Drove, Fengate – three kilometres (two miles) east of Peterborough – includes reconstructed Bronze and Iron Age roundhouses and a museum containing the oldest wheel in England.

It features an archaeological park with working excavations (at Easter and all through Summer).

There are also rare breeds which match periods of pre-history – including Moufflon, Shetland and Soay sheep, pigs which are a cross between wild boars and Tamworth pigs derived from the Iron Age, as well as Exmoor and Shetland ponies.

The site was originally discovered in 1982 – when a mechanical digger working on fenland drainage pulled up some timber, which appeared to

have been split in a very distinctive manner.

The site, which includes a gift shop and refreshment facilities, is open between 10am and 5pm daily, except for the Christmas and New Year period.

National Dragonfly Museum

The museum – at Ashton Mill, almost a kilometre (half a mile) south of the Oundle roundabout on the Peterborough to Northampton Road – is unique in Europe and one of only two in the world.

It is open between 10.30am and 5pm on Saturdays, Sundays and Bank Holiday Mondays from mid-June to late September.

Nene Park

Passengers disembarking from the Nene Valley railway (See below) at **Ferry Meadows** can enjoy the Nene country park's many attractions, including boat trips, children's play areas, cycle hire, golf, a miniature railway, nature trails, pony rides and water sports.

A café, picnic site, shops and visitor centre are also on site.

Nene Valley Railway

Featured in many TV and film productions – one of the Bond films involved the hero in a roof-level chase along its carriages – this famous 24 kilometre (15-mile) long railway runs through the Nene Country Park.

From its eastern terminus at Peterborough's Nene Valley station –

Flag Fen roundhouses

a mere 20 minutes walk from the city centre – it extends west through its Wansford Station headquarters, through the supposedly haunted Wansford tunnel to Yarwell junction.

Wansford itself is home to a unique collection of historic locomotives and coaches from both Britain and Europe (open on most operating days) as well as a café, book shop and gift shop.

Market Deeping

A triangular town centre features several inns and guest houses with large archways, which recall the days when horse-drawn carriages and stage coaches stopped here.

The nearby unspoiled small village of Deeping St James is charming and features several locks making river access to Stamford possible by controlling height and flow.

Peakirk Waterfowl World

Hundreds of birds from around the world inhabit the eight hectares (20 acres) of gardens, waterways and woodland of this visitor attraction at Deeping Road, Peakirk.

It features a tea room and is open between 9.30am and 5.30pm from March to October and between 10am and dusk from November to February.

Prebendal Manor House

The 13th century manor at Nassington, 12 kilometres (eight miles) west of Peterborough, is the oldest manor in Northamptonshire and is Grade 1 listed.

Prebendal, which has experienced occasional ghostly apparitions, also boasts the largest 14th century medieval garden in Europe – it extends to 2.5 hectares (six acres) and is unique to the region.

Features include a rose tunnel arbour, dovecote, herber, turf seats, fountain, medieval kitchen garden, tree seat, tree arbour, medieval fish ponds and a vineyard.

The manor house – where lunches and home-made teas are available in the tithe barn – is open between 1pm and 5.30pm on Wednesdays and Sundays in May,

Rutland Water

June and September.

Additionally, visitors are admitted between the same times on Thursdays in July and August as well as all Bank Holidays.

Rutland Water

Some 32 kilometres (20 miles) north-east of Peterborough, at the heart of England's smallest county – Rutland – is the largest man-made lake in Western Europe.

It offers panoramic views and rural tranquillity – along with a butterfly and aquatic centre, cycling and walking opportunities, lake cruises, a Norman church and watersports.

Normanton Church, formerly part of the Normanton Estate, now stands, half submerged, on the edge of Rutland Water.

Today, it houses a display dedicated to the creation of the reservoir and history of the area and a video of the construction is shown.

Rutland Water Nature Reserve, at the north end of the reservoir, is designated a Site of Special Scientific Interest (SSSI).

It is a regular host to internationally important numbers of gadwall and shoveller ducks, together with a Winter population of 20,000 water birds.

Rutland is also playing a major part in efforts to reintroduce the fish-eating osprey into England – it has not bred in this country for 150 years.

However, there are signs that a 'translocation plan' – involving chicks being brought from nests in the Scottish Highlands and placed in specially-designed release pens on raised platforms at Rutland – may lead to success.

The Butterfly and Aquatic

Peakirk Waterfowl World
Tel. 01733 252271

Prebendal Manor House
e-mail: info@prebendal-manor.demon.co.uk
web: www.prebendal-manor.demon.co.uk

Rutland Butterfly and Aquatic Centre
Tel. 01780 460515

Rutland cycling
Tel. 01780 460705
web:
www.rutlandcycling.co.uk

Rutland Outdoor Climbing and Activity Centre
Tel. 01780 460060

Rutland Water
Tel. 01780 460321

Rutland Water fishing bookings
Tel. 01780 686441
24-hour fishing line
01780 686442
Fishing Lodge
Tel. 01780 686443

Rutland Water Nature Reserve
Tel. 01572 770651
Fax. 01572 755931
e-mail: awbc@rutlandwater.org.uk
web: www.rutlandwater.u-net.com

Rutland Watersports Centre
Tel. 01780 460154

Rutland Water Tourist Information Centre
Tel. 01572 653026
web: www.anglian.co.uk/environment/env_rutland.htm

Centre, next to the Tourist Information Centre, is a 464 square metre (5,000 square feet) glasshouse and the 'rainforest atmosphere' is home to many brilliantly coloured butterflies from all over the globe.

The Centre is open between 10.30am and 5pm from April to August, and 10.30am to 4.30pm from September to October (Closed during Winter).

Over 810 hectares (2,000 acres) of water is available for sailing, windsurfing, and canoeing.

Huge rainbow and brown trout are caught at Rutland, which has a reputation as one of the finest fisheries in Europe.

The 'Rutland Belle' takes visitors on a 45-minute pleasure cruise around the reservoir. A total of 75 passengers can be accommodated in all weather conditions and there is an upper sun deck for 35 additional passengers.

Sacrewell Farm and Country Centre

Sacrewell at Thornaugh, north-west of Peterborough, features agricultural bygones, gardens, gift shop, miller's kitchen, nature trails, picnic area, visitor centre, working farm and working watermill.

It is open daily all year round from 9.30am to 5pm.

Sacrewell Farm
Tel./Fax. 01780 782254
e-mail: sacrewell@
peterborough.net

George Hotel, Stamford
Tel. 01780 750750
Fax. 01780 750701
e-mail: reservations@
georgehotelofstamford.com
web: www.georgehotel
ofstamford.com

Stamford Museum
Tel. 01780 766317

Stamford Arts Centre
Tel. 01780 763203

Burghley House
Tel. 01780 752451
Fax. 01780 480125
web: www.stamford.
co.uk/burghley/

Tallington Lakes
Tel. 01778 347000 or
344990

**Thorney Abbey &
Heritage Centre**
Tel. 01733 270908

Whittlesey Museum
Tel. 01733 840968

Stamford

The beauty and charm of this historic Georgian town has changed little over the centuries.

Famous for its hills, winding roads and cobbled side streets, Stamford and its townscape – there are more than 600 listed buildings and no fewer than five Medieval churches – once drew notable praise from Sir Walter Scott.

In the centre of town, on what was once the Great North Road from London to York, stands **The George Hotel** – a hostelry believed to have belonged to the Abbots of Croyland (Crowland) some 900 or so years ago.

During the 17th and 18th centuries, when England's roads became busier than ever before, the ancient coaching inn was frequented by royalty and nobility – with King Charles I and William III among its guests.

One of its biggest customers, however, was Daniel Lambert, whose portrait and walking stick can be seen in the hotel. For Lambert, the largest man ever to live, weighed 335 kilograms (52 stone 11 lbs) when he died in 1809 at the age of 39!

Stamford Museum, in Broad Street (usually open 10am to 5pm) also has a memento of Lambert, in the form of a display of his clothes.

The town, which has featured in many films and TV series – the award-winning Middlemarch was shot here – also boasts an 18th century **arts centre** and open-air theatre and renowned stained glass in its All Saints Church.

Nearby **Burghley House** (open daily between 11am and 4.30pm from Easter to early October), was

The George Hotel, Stamford

built by Elizabeth 1st's Lord High Treasurer in the 16th century and has been the home of the Cecil family for over 400 years.

Burghley, whose gardens and park were landscaped by the celebrated 'Capability' Brown, is now the home of Lady Victoria Leatham and her family.

The annual horse trials, held in the park, attract competitors and visitors from all over the world.

Tallington Lakes

A dry ski slope and a variety of water sports facilities are to be found within this 64 hectare (160-acre) naturally spring-fed site between Market Deeping and Stamford.

There is also a camping and caravanning site, Lakeside bar and restaurant.

Thorney Abbey & Heritage Centre

Located north-east of Peterborough, these two Thorney sites (open between 2 and 5pm at week-ends only from Easter to the end of September) offer bookable tours.

The Heritage museum features the development of the site from monastic days, taking in Walloon and Flemish influences, drainage and model housing for which the Duke of Bedford was responsible.

Whittlesey

Situated on the western edge of the Fens, Whittlesey features an interesting maze of streets in its town centre – as well as some rare thatched mud walls.

The town was one of the last places in the country where the old agricultural custom of Straw Bear dancing took place – and this Plough Monday (January) tradition, revived in 1980, has grown to become a unique feast of entertainment.

Among exhibits in the **museum** (open on Saturday mornings and Friday and Sunday afternoons) are the contents of a 1950s village post office and mementoes of soldier Sir Harry Smith, a 19th century resident of the town.

Huntingdon town centre

Huntingdon

The origins of Huntingdon go back to Paleolithic and Neolithic times and there was a Bronze Age burial site at Brampton.

Oliver Cromwell was born in the town in 1599 and is remembered through several of its buildings.

The font used for his baptism is in All Saints' Church (which also contains his family burial vault) and his father – Robert Cromwell – was one of two bailiffs who contributed towards the cost of repairing St Mary's Church in 1609.

The Cromwell Museum – housed in the former grammar school attended by both the Lord Protector and diarist Samuel Pepys (who lived at Brampton) – is the only dedicated collection in the country and contains an extensive collection of family portraiture.

Hinchingbrooke House, a Tudor country residence now part of Hinchingbrooke School, opens to the public every Sunday afternoon from the early Bank Holiday to the late August Bank Holiday.

Huntingdon Area

Fenland Light Railway

A narrow gauge miniature steam railway, which is located at Ramsey Mereside and holds 'steaming' days once a month from May to October.

Grafham Water

Grafham, owned by Anglian Water, was created in the mid-1960s as a supply reservoir.

The 150-hectare (370-acre) nature reserve situated along its western shores is managed in partnership with The Wildlife Trust for Cambridgeshire (Tel. 01223 846363).

The site, through which a cycling route and walk pass, features four bird hides – two of which have access for the disabled.

There is also a wildlife garden, a dragonfly pond, four nature trails and two woodland areas, called Littless Wood and Savages Spinney.

The Harbour View restaurant is open from 7am until late, seven days a week, from April to October and from 9.30am to 5.30pm during the winter months.

Grafham Water Centre

The Centre, on the southern shores of Grafham Water, was established 30 years ago and is owned and run by Cambridgeshire County Council.

It offers residential and non-residential courses in a wide range of water and land-based activities – including canoeing, kayaking, powerboating, sailing, windsurfing, abseiling and climbing, archery, mountain biking and orienteering.

Hamerton Zoo Park

Set in six hectares (15 acres) of parkland at Hamerton, just outside Huntingdon, the park (open daily except Christmas Day) specialises in breeding programmes for rare and endangered species.

It is home to more than a hundred species of exotic birds and animals from all over the world.

Hamerton Zoo Park

Cromwell Museum
Tel. 01480 375830

Hinchingbrooke House
Tel. 01480 375678

Fenland Light Railway
Tel. 01733 844615

Grafham Water
(Angling bookings)
Tel. 01480 810531

Grafham Water Centre
Tel. 01480 810521
Fax. 01480 812739
web: www.camcnty.gov.uk/
sub/grafham

Hamerton Zoo Park
Tel. 01832 293362

Hinchingbrooke
Country Park
Tel. 01480 451568

Houghton Mill
Tel. 01480 301494
Fax. 01480 469641

Hinchingbrooke Country Park

The park –just west of Huntingdon, off the A14 – covers 72.84 hectares (180 acres) of woodland, grassland, flower meadows, lakes and ponds.

There is also a Romano-British Village – built six years ago for educational purposes – which vividly illustrates what country life was like when Iron Age Briton met Roman invader and settler some two thousand years ago.

The visitor centre – where disabled parking is available and there are battery-powered wheelchairs available for use – is staffed seven-days-a-week and the café is open at peak times.

Houghton Mill

An impressive, working 17th century water mill on the River Ouse at Houghton, east of Huntingdon.

Milling still takes place on Sundays and Bank Holiday Mondays and there are miniature millstones to turn by hand.

Other features include children's interactivities and a gallery showing the work of local artists.

The mill is open between 2 and 5.30pm daily (except Thursday and Friday) from the end of June to the beginning of September and at weekends and Bank Holiday Mondays from the beginning of April to late June and the beginning of September to the beginning of October.

Island Hall

A mid-18th century Godmanchester mansion, originally built by the Receiver General for Huntingdon, restored after a fire in 1978 and now privately owned.

The house, which can be visited by arrangement, is located in a tranquil riverside setting with formal gardens and an ornamental island.

National Hunt Racing

Some 18 meetings are held during the season at Huntingdon Steeplechases, Brampton.

Paxton Pits

This valuable Site of Special Scientific Interest, a short way down the road from Grafham Water, consists of flooded gravel workings.

The land in, and to the north of, Little Paxton was farmland until the aggregates industry found that it was rich in sand and gravel.

Many of the former workings, which were dug out between the 1940s and early 1960s, have been turned over to wildlife and are now an important haven for birds, mammals, flowers and insects.

The Pits complex is home to almost a quarter of the county's nightingales and has one of the largest inland colonies of cormorants in Britain as well as several nation-

Huntingdon racecourse

ally scarce plants – such as the great dodder.

The Paxton Pits Nature reserve is open to the public all day, every day, and is a good starting point for the Ouse Valley Way.

A detailed map in the car park shows the trails and footpaths around the reserve and leaflets and maps are available from the visitor centre.

The visitor centre is open most Sundays and at other busy times, often offers light refreshments and has toilet facilities which are equally suitable for people who are disabled.

Ramsey Abbey and Gatehouse

The Benedictine Abbey founded by Ailwyn in 969 AD became one of the most important in England during the 12th and 13th centuries.

After the Dissolution in 1539, the Abbey and all its lands were sold to Oliver Cromwell's great grandfather and most of the buildings were demolished.

Stonework from Ramsey was used, however, to build Caius, Kings and Trinity colleges at Cambridge, the towers of Ramsey, Godmanchester and Holywell churches, the gate at Hinchingbrooke House and several local houses.

What may have been the mid-13th century Lady Chapel was incorporated by the Cromwells into Hinchingbrooke House (q.v.) around 1600 and subsequently greatly extended.

At Ramsey only the porter's lodge of what was a magnificent 15th century Purbeck marble gatehouse survives today – the actual gateway having been taken down and rebuilt to form the principal entrance to the outer court at Hinchingbrooke House.

The richly-carved remains – which contain, on the ground floor, an effigy of Ailwyn – now belong to the National Trust and are open daily to visitors between 10am and 5pm from the beginning of April to the end of October.

Ramsey Abbey and Gatehouse

Ramsey Rural Museum

The museum displays traditional implements used by local craftsmen such as cobblers, dairymen, farriers, thatchers and wheelwrights.

It contains many old machines which were used to work the reclaimed fenland and have now been restored to their former glory.

The museum, which also houses a collection of local bygones and old photographs, is open between 2 and 5pm Thursday to Sunday from April to September.

Raptor Foundation

Known formerly as Ramsey Raptor Rescue, Cambridgeshire's Bird of Prey Hospital is based on an eight hectare (20-acre) site at St Ives Road, Woodhurst – between St Ives and Somersham.

As well as being home to some 350 birds of prey – mostly injured, orphaned or unwanted – the Foundation features an art gallery, children's play area, flower garden, picnic area and tearoom.

The site is open between 10.30am and 5pm all year round and there are regular falconry displays (subject to weather).

St Ives

The present town began life in Anglo-Saxon days as 'Slepe', where the River Great Ouse could be crossed at a ford in the 7th century.

The change of name came around 800 years ago as a result of the mysterious St Ivo – said to have been a Persian bishop who came to this country as a Christian missionary and died at Slepe in the 7th century.

A priory (of which a few traces can

still be seen) was built on the site where his bones, which were alleged to have healing properties, were discovered some 1000 years ago.

Pilgrims started visiting the priory, merchants and traders arrived to seek their custom and a town grew up around the site of Easter and August fairs granted by charter from King Henry 1st and King John.

Interesting features of the modern town include the Cromwell Statue on Market Hill, commemorating the Roundhead leader's residence at St Ives from 1631–36.

The Chapel of St Leger, in the middle of the river bridge, dates back to the 15th century and is one of only four bridge chapels in the country.

At one time, in the 18th century, when the chapel was used as a house, two brick storeys were added – but these were removed when the chapel was restored to its original form in 1930.

Although not now used for regular worship, the chapel is still home to church services from time to time.

Visits are possible by obtaining a key from the town hall or **Norris Museum,** which is the museum of Huntingdonshire and tells the story of the development of the county from the days of dinosaurs to the present time.

Interesting fittings in All Saints' Church – part of which dates back to the 12th century – include a 13th century font, an Elizabethan pulpit and a vast 19th century organ.

The nearby 12th century Manor of **Hemingford Grey** is one of the oldest continuously inhabited homes in England and was immortalised by author Lucy Boston (who bought the property in the 1930s) as the house of Green Knowe in her series of children's classics.

The gardens are open between 10am and 6pm daily (sunset in winter) but visits to the house, which contains a collection of exquisite patchworks, are strictly by appointment only.

St Neots

This pretty market town – the largest in Cambridgeshire – also dates back to Saxon times, when a priory was founded on the outskirts of Eynsbury in 974 AD.

Its name comes from a Cornish saint, whose remains were interred there some time before the Norman Conquest.

A first Great Ouse bridge, built in 1180 and consisting of 73 timber arches, contributed much to the town's importance and prosperity and the stone structure which replaced it around 1600 was the scene of a battle between the Roundheads and Royalists in 1648.

The magnificent St Neots parish church of St Mary the Virgin is known locally as the Cathedral of Huntingdonshire and contains a 17th century carved oak altar, excellent Victorian glass and a 19th century Holdich organ.

Examples of late Norman work can be seen in the 14th century oak benches in Eynsbury parish church, which also features a 17th century pulpit and the grave of the 8 foot plus, so-called 'Eynsbury Giant' – James Toller.

The new, award-winning St Neots **Museum** – housed in the former Magistrates' Court, police station and original 1907 cell block – tells the story of the town from prehistoric times.

The museum is open between 10.30am and 4.30pm from Wednesday to Saturday.

Nearby **Buckden Towers,** where Catherine of Aragon was imprisoned prior to the annulment of her marriage to Henry VIII, features a 15th century gatehouse and Great Tower as well as a recreated Tudor garden.

Wood Green Animal Shelter

The famous shelter, at Kings Bush Farm, has been visited for two Anglia series about the animals and the people who look after them.

The purpose-built centre, which is open to the public every day of the year except Christmas Day, boasts a restaurant, arena for special events and a pleasant nature trail.

Narrow-boating through St Neots

Island Hall
Tel. 0207 491 3724

**Huntingdon
Steeplechases**
Tel. 01480 453373

**Paxton Pits
Nature Reserve**
Tel. 01480 406795
web: www.paxton-pits.org.uk

**Ramsey Abbey and
Gatehouse**
Tel. 01263 733471

Ramsey Rural Museum
Tel. 01487 814304 or
815715

Raptor Foundation
Tel. 01487 741140
e-mail: raptor.foundation@
tesco.net
web: http://homepages.
tesco.net/~raptor.foundation

Chapel of St Leger
Tel. 01480 497314

Norris Museum
Tel. 01480 497314

Hemingford Grey
Tel. 01480 463134

St Neots Museum
Tel. 01480 388788 or
388921

Buckden Towers
Tel. 01480 810344

**Wood Green
Animal Shelter**
Tel. 01480 830014
Fax. 01480 830158

South Cambridgeshire

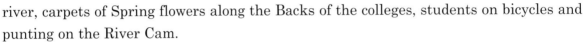

Over 3½ million people each year visit the world-renowned University City of Cambridge, which combines an ancient history with a recently-acquired reputation for technological and scientific excellence.

For many people Cambridge conjures up images of the magnificent King's College Chapel, viewed from across the river, carpets of Spring flowers along the Backs of the colleges, students on bicycles and punting on the River Cam.

Beyond its limits, the city is surrounded on all sides by heritage towns and villages.

ℹ Tourist Information Centres

Cambridge
Tel. 01223 322640; Fax. 01223 457588
e-mail: tourism@cambridge.gov.uk
web: www.cambridge.gov.uk

Ordnance Survey Maps
OS Landranger sheet number: 154

The Bridge of Sighs and St John's College, Cambridge

Cambridge

This bustling city of over 109,000 people was important long before the University existed.

For here, at the meeting of dense forests to the south and trackless, marshy Fens to the north, there was the lowest reliable fording place of the River Cam, or Granta.

In the first century BC an Iron Age Belgic tribe built a settlement on what is now Castle Hill. Around AD40 the Romans took over the site and it became the crossing point for the Via Devana which linked Colchester with the legions in Lincoln and beyond.

The Saxons followed, then the Normans under William the Conqueror, who raised a castle on a steep mound as a base for fighting the Saxon rebel, Hereward the Wake, deep in the Fens at Ely.

The motte of William's castle still stands and Ely Cathedral is visible from the top on a clear day.

ADC Theatre

The oldest playhouse in England specialises in quality drama, mainly from student companies but local and touring productions are also featured.

Boat Race

A friendly and intimate live performance venue open in the city centre's East Road a full seven nights a week.

On the music menu is everything from acoustic to ambient, blues to country and indie to jazz.

Botanic Garden

This magnificent garden, served by an early 17th watercourse bringing chalk spring water down from the Gog Magog Hills, is at Cambridge University.

The 16-hectare (40-acre) garden was established in 1831 as a university teaching and research resource and is located close to Cambridge railway station, off Hills Road.

It centres on a splendid lake and contains one of the finest limestone

Cambridge Botanic Garden

☎ FAX 🖥

ADC Theatre
information
Tel. 01223 359547
booking
Tel. 01223 503333

Boat Race
Tel. 01223 508533
e-mail: stan@
boatrace.cambsnet.co.uk or
paul@scar.cambsnet.co.uk

Botanic Garden
Tel. 01223 336265
guided tours
Tel. 01223 336271

Cherry Hinton Village Centre
Tel. 01223 576412

rock gardens anywhere in the world, with all its plants arranged geographically.

There are many superb trees, too, including a 22.2 metre (72 ft 6 in) Dawn Redwood, which came from the seed of a species rediscovered in China in 1946 and is now one of the prize specimens in the country.

Cambridge is also famous for its huge range of more than a hundred families of hardy herbaceous plants.

But perhaps the garden, right the middle of the busy university town, is best known for its national geranium collection, boasting many newer, rarer species.

For future generations of students there are conservation beds of wild native flowers and grasses – like The Corn Cockle, the Hairy Greenwood and the Furrow-wax – all of which might soon disappear.

There's also a newly-established genetic garden and a wonderful scented garden which explodes into life in May and June to delight the blind particularly.

But the garden as a whole is a year-round attraction and it can now look at its most stunning in Winter and early Spring – thanks to the Winter Garden designed by Norman Villis and added in the last few years.

The Botanic Garden is open between at least 10am and 3.45pm

daily except on Christmas Day and Boxing Day.

Guided tours are available by arrangement and facilities on site include light refreshments and a shop.

Cherry Hinton Village Centre

A well-equipped sports and community centre which is in the heart of Cherry Hinton and is often used to hold a wide variety of public fairs and bazaars.

Churches

The memorial to Godfrey Washington in Little St Mary's bears stars and stripes and is said to be the origin of the United States flag.

The church of St Bene't is the oldest in Cambridgeshire and features an Anglo-Saxon tower.

Cambridge market

The Round Church is, as its name would imply, round – and one of only four of its kind surviving in England.

Colleges

The first scholars didn't arrive in Cambridge until 1209 and another 75 years passed before Hugh de Balsham, Bishop of Ely, founded the first college – Peterhouse.

Clare (1326), Pembroke (1347), Gonville and Caius (1348), Trinity Hall (1350) and Corpus Christi (1352) were established in the first half of the fourteenth century.

Ten more colleges were founded during the fifteenth and sixteenth centuries – including Christ's (1505), King's (1441), Queens' (1448), Jesus (1496), St. John's (1511), Trinity (1546), and Emmanuel (1584).

Henry VI took nearly a quarter of the medieval city for King's College and Henry VIII united two existing colleges to make Trinity grand enough to rival Christ Church in the 'Other Place'.

Women didn't have a proper college until Girton (founded in 1869) opened in 1873.

There are now 31 colleges – the latest, Robinson College, founded in 1977 by a local millionaire.

King's College, Cambridge

Cambridge Round Church
Tel. 01223 871621 or
0831 839261

Corn Exchange
Tel. 01223 357851
Fax. 01223 329074
e-mail: boxoffice@
cambridge.gov.uk
web: www.cornex.co.uk

Darkroom Gallery
Tel. 01223 566725

Drama Centre (information)
Tel. 01223 322748

Eagle public house
Tel. 01223 505020

Guide Friday Bus Tours
Tel. 01233 362444
web: www.guidefriday.com/
tours.html

Corn Exchange

This Wheeler Street concert venue is housed in a Grade II* listed building which was closed for six weeks during the Summer of 2000.

That was for a major £100,000 scheme to install lift access to both the boxes and second floor bar and also provide a ramped access from the front of the building to the café and auditorium.

The work, however, was due to be completed in time for a hectic and varied Autumn 2000 season.

Darkroom Gallery

An ongoing programme of exhibitions, workshops and events combines with public facilities for

Trinity College, Cambridge

darkroom work and digital imaging.

Work by a variety of international as well as regional photographers is often on show.

The Gwydir Street gallery is open between 12 noon and 5pm from Tuesday to Sunday.

Drama Centre

A lively Covent Garden, Mill Road studio venue which operates both as a theatre for contemporary touring productions and a workshop space.

Eagle

This pub at Benet Street, Cambridge, has a famous ceiling on which British and Allied airmen from the last World War used candle smoke to write their names and inscriptions, which can still be clearly seen.

Opening times are between 11am and 11pm from Monday to Saturday and from 12 noon to 10.30pm on Sundays.

Guide Friday Bus Tours

'Hop-on, hop-off' bus offering guided sightseeing tours of Cambridge and the American Cemetery. Tickets valid all day.

Buses run daily, though less frequently in Winter.

Junction

A busy Clifton Road entertainment centre which can feature an all-night club one night, a gig the next and contemporary dance the night after.

The venue features a café and several bars on two levels.

Kettle's Yard

A Castle Street art gallery which stages several 20th century exhibitions each year and houses, in a domestic setting, a permanent collection containing 20th century art and sculpture along with natural objects, furniture and decorative arts.

Works by Henry Moore, Ben Nicholson, Alfred Wallis, Henry Gaudier Brzeska and Barbara Hepworth are included.

The house at Kettle's Yard is open between 2pm and 4pm daily (except Mondays and Bank Holidays) and the gallery between 12.30pm and 5.30pm from Tuesday to Saturday and 2pm and 5pm on Sundays.

Museums

The Trumpington Street **Fitzwilliam,** started in 1834, is the grandest and most renowned of several excellent university museums.

It houses one of the finest art collections in Great Britain, including a magnificent permanent exhibition of paintings, decorative arts and antiquities in splendid 19th century buildings.

The Fitzwilliam is owned and run by the University of Cambridge and is open between 10am and 5pm from Tuesday to Saturday and between 2.15pm and 5pm on Sundays.

The Castle Street **Folk Museum,** filled with Cambridgeshire bygones, is open between 10.30am and 5pm from Tuesday to Saturday and 2pm and 5pm on Sundays throughout the year and, additionally, on Mondays (10.30am–5pm) from April to September.

The Museum of Zoology features specimens of insects, land mammals and sea mammals and is open from 2.15pm from Monday to Friday.

Scott Polar Research Institute

Punting on the River Cam, Cambridge

is a museum of polar life and exploration and is usually open between 2.30pm and 4pm from Monday to Saturday (But please check for current times).

The Sedgwick Museum (open between 9am and 5pm, with an hour's lunch break, from Monday to Friday and 10am–1pm on Saturdays) has an extensive collection of geological specimens.

The University Museum of Archaeology and Anthropology (open between 2pm and 4pm from Monday to Friday) illustrates prehistoric and recent traditional cultures from all parts of the world as well as local archaeology.

University Museum of Classical Archaeology features plaster casts of Greek and Roman sculptures and is open between 9am and 5pm from Monday to Friday.

The comprehensive collection of scientific instruments at Whipple Museum of Science can be viewed between 2pm and 4pm from Monday to Friday throughout the year and between the same times on Saturdays as well from May to November.

NB. Some museums may be closed during the university holidays.

Punting

There are few better ways to take in the sights of Cambridge than by punting down the Cam.

Punting for pleasure developed at Cambridge in 1902 from flat-bottomed boats which were used to move goods around in the shallow waters of The Fens.

There are two rivers which can be explored by punt from Cambridge – the Upper River (which winds behind the colleges, or Backs) and the Granta, which flows out to Granchester.

☎ **FAX** **🖳**

Junction
Tel. 01223 511511
e-mail: bookings@
junction.co.uk

Kettle's Yard
Tel. 01223 352124

Fitzwilliam Museum
Tel. 01223 332900

Folk Museum
Tel. 01223 355159

Museum of Zoology
Tel. 01223 336650

Scott Polar Research Institute
Tel. 01223 336540

Sedgwick Museum, Downing Site
Tel. 01223 333456

University Museum of Archaeology and Anthropology
Tel. 01223 333516

University Museum of Classical Archaeology
Tel. 01223 335153

Whipple Museum of Classical Archaeology
Tel. 01223 334540

The Fitzwilliam Museum, Cambridge

Places of interest to be seen along the way include:

Queens' College and its famous wooden mathematical bridge.

King's College with its sandstone buildings.

King's College Chapel – which houses Rubens' Adoration of the Magi and is, perhaps, the most dramatic building along The Backs.

Clare Bridge – the only one

available for Oliver Cromwell to use to cross into Cambridge during The Civil War.

Garett Hostel bridge, which is modelled on a gull's wing and won an award for its modern, lightweight design.

Trinity College – where the young Prince Charles studied and there is the magnificent Georgian-style library designed by Sir Christopher Wren.

St John's College – nicknamed 'the wedding cake' – where Wordsworth had rooms.

Kitchen Bridge, whose stone-work records the highest-ever flood level in Cambridge (in 1947).

The covered Bridge of Sighs – based on the original in Venice, linking the courtrooms with the prison. Cambridge's version separates the exam rooms and the accommodation for students – prompting sighs of relief as they cross it!

Magdalene Bridge – nicknamed Quayside.

Scudamore's Punting Company, which has 150 punts and can be found at Granta Place, Mill Lane, Cambridge (next to Garden House Hotel), is open from Easter to October.

West Road Concert Hall

A 500-seater venue designed by the architect of London's Festival Hall and renowned for its acoustical qualities and comfort.

The hall serves as a major venue for classical music for both town and gown and stages events throughout the year.

Anglesey Abbey

Cambridge Area

American Cemetery

The Cemetery is one of 14 permanent American WWII military memorials erected on foreign soil by the American Battle Monuments Commission.

It is open daily throughout the year between 8am and 5pm and there is no entrance charge.

Anglesey Abbey

It's hard to believe the famous garden of the Abbey, with its curious mix of 17th century French and 19th century English influences, was actually designed and planted less than a hundred years ago.

Anglesey, just off A10 Cambridge to Ely road, north east of Cambridge, was the creation of the First Lord Fairhaven, Huttleston Broughton.

He bought Anglesey and its then relatively compact garden in 1926 so that he could be near his stud and the racing at Newmarket.

Broughton then set about investing into the development of the house and grounds the huge fortunes he'd inherited from his father, an American rail and oil magnate.

The bulk of Lord Fairhaven's new estate was described as 'uninspiring fen' – but for him it was a blank canvas on which he could paint his vision of a quintessential English garden.

He mixed the disciplines of the formal and the informal to create a garden made up of the best of the past.

At the far north of the grounds by the Lode Mill – bought by Lord Fairhaven in 1934 and restored to working order in 1982 (demonstrations on the first Saturday of each month) – you could be in yet another garden, in another world.

The house at Anglesey Abbey is probably best known for its outstanding

Chilford Hundred Vineyard

collection of works of art. Not all, though, are contained within its walls.

For the gardens are home to one of the largest collections of ornamental statuary in England – much of it tucked away, almost hidden from view.

Maintaining the unusual garden and its statues is not easy. But it's carried out faithfully in honour of Lord Fairhaven, who bequeathed the property to the National Trust in 1966.

The historian Sir Arthur Bryant wrote of him: "Lord Fairhaven must be almost unique...

"With patience, single-minded devotion and flawless taste, in an age of war and revolution, he has endowed the England of tomorrow with a landscape garden worthy of her past."

Anglesey Abbey is open between 1 and 5pm from mid-March to mid-October (Wed–Sun and Bank Holiday Monday afternoon) with the gardens alone open daily from early July to mid-September and from at least Thursday to Sunday at other times of the year (check for details).

On site there are refreshments, a shop, toilets, and, in the gardens only, disabled facilities.

Burwell Museum and Windmill

The museum is attractively housed in a group of reconstructed historical buildings, which were re-opened in 1992 and contain representations of life in the area over the past century.

The site, north east of Cambridge, is open between 2pm and 5pm on Thursdays, Sundays and Bank Holiday Mondays from Easter until the end of September.

There are special events once a

month on Sunday afternoons and Bank Holidays.

Chilford Hundred Vineyard

This seven hectare (18-acre) vineyard and winery at Linton is the largest in Cambridgeshire – as well as Norfolk and Suffolk.

Located east of Cambridge, it is open between 11am and 5.30pm throughout the week from the beginning of March to immediately before Christmas.

Tours are conducted daily on the hour between 11am and 4pm until the end of October – and, by arrangement, from then on until pre-Christmas closing.

Admission includes a tour of the winery, wine tasting and a souvenir glass.

Chilford's wines are exported to America, France, Holland and Norway and its flagship Aluric de Norsehide – a sparkling pink – has been recommended by Jilly Goolden and Good Food Magazine.

On site there is a café and gift shop, which sells Chilford wines and speciality foods, and the vineyard is part of an interesting group of barns and buildings, sculpture and monumental masonry.

Classic Wings

Based at the Imperial War Museum at Duxford (q.v.), Classic Wings offers flights in 1930s De Havilland Dragon Rapides over Cambridge and Madingley, Cambridge, Ely and Newmarket or London.

The company, which also arranges flights in Tiger Moths, is open between 10am and 6pm daily from April to October.

Denny Abbey

Farmland Museum & Denny Abbey

The Farmland Museum, which brings traditional rural crafts to life, is in the grounds of Denny Abbey at Chittering, near Waterbeach – 10 kilometres (six miles) north of Cambridge.

The Abbey, an attractive, stone-built farmhouse, is actually the remains of a 12th century Benedictine building, which was once home to the Knights Templar, Franciscan nuns and the Countess of Pembroke.

The museum itself focuses on the farming of the region and its collection of over 6000 objects includes photographs, machinery and tools from rural crafts and industries – all made and used by Cambridgeshire people.

A barn houses larger farming equipment and renovated pig sheds contain a dairy, a blacksmith's and basket-maker's workshops.

The museum offers 'hands-on' activities – including butter-making and basket-making workshops – to make the various equipment and machinery accessible to younger generations possibly unfamiliar with farming.

The larger churns on display in the dairy are late 19th century – although hand-made butter making is an ancient practice.

The surrounding fenland area has a history of dairy products – especially the cheese-making village of Cottenham, from which Samuel Pepys' family hailed.

The Farmland Museum & Denny Abbey is at Ely Road, Waterbeach, and is open daily between 12 noon and 5pm from the beginning of April to the end of October.

There's a programme of special events throughout the season and educational parties can phone and book.

Imperial War Museum

This historic former RAF Battle of Britain airfield, at Duxford, south of Cambridge, is now Europe's premier aviation museum.

Its outstanding collection of more

Imperial War Museum, Duxford

than 180 historic aircraft ranges from biplanes to Comet and Concorde.

Duxford is part of the Imperial War Museum and is the centre for historic aviation.

Rare aircraft such as Spitfires and Mustangs regularly fly from the airfield and participate in air displays, which are held throughout the Summer months.

Also featured is a restored Battle of Britain operations room, an American Air Museum and a Land Warfare Hall, displaying tanks and military vehicles in authentic battleground scenes.

A free courtesy bus runs daily from Cambridge.

Duxford is open between 10am and 4pm daily from the end of October to mid-March and between 10am and 6pm for the remainder of the year.

Linton Zoo

Named in the 1999 Good Guide to Britain as Cambridgeshire's Family Attraction of the Year, Linton Zoological Gardens, near Cambridge, was established by the Simmons family.

They left a thriving pet shop and zoo suppliers' business in 1972 to set up a wildlife-breeding centre out of "love, interest and concern for the wildlife of the world."

Linton is noted for its beautiful gardens, which cover 6.5 hectares (16 acres). Over 10,000 bedding plants are put in every year and there are unusual trees and shrubs such as fan palms, Tasmanian giant tree ferns and Chinese trumpet vines.

During Summer thousands of butterflies visit the gardens and breed on the wild plants, which are left especially for them.

Big cats include two amur, or Siberian tigers, from Russian and German zoos, a lioness, a breeding pair of snow leopards, two female leopards and a male black leopard –

Linton Zoo

also known as a panther, but actually a black variant of the normal spotted type and not a separate species.

Smaller members of the cat family include Siberian and caracal lynxes. Like their smaller, domesticated cousins, wild cats spend much of their time sleeping, especially in hot weather.

Linton has eating and souvenir outlets as well as a covered picnic space, children's play area and a bouncy castle in fine weather.

Keeper talks, animal encounters and a full activity programme are also available to the public.

The zoo's fun family Quiz Trail is always available – ask for sheets at the gate. Proceeds from Quiz Trail sheets support the Conservation Fund.

There are Shetland pony rides – for children weighing less than 25 kilograms (four stones) – throughout the school holidays and busy weekends, weather permitting.

Linton is open daily, except for Christmas Day, from 10am to 6pm (or dusk, if earlier) with last admissions one hour before closing time.

There is disabled access to all areas and dogs, although not allowed in the zoo, can be walked in a lane nearby.

Milton Country Park

A 34 hectare (85-acre) country park located north-east of Cambridge and consisting of woodland, grass and water areas.

There is a network of paths for cyclists and walkers as well as a marked trail for horse riders.

Wicken Fen

Wicken, some 16 kilometres (10 miles) from Ely, Newmarket and Cambridge, is Britain's oldest nature reserve and home to rare species including hen harriers and bitterns.

It is one of the very few remaining original parts of the Great Fen of East Anglia – now largely drained and given over to arable farmland.

The level of the soil surface fell with drainage and this has left Wicken Sedge Fen as 'an island',

Wicken Fen

standing up to two metres above the surrounding countryside.

Because it was never drained or ploughed, the fen, reeds and wet greenland are a refuge for many species of plants and animals far more abundant many years ago.

Just under a hectare (two acres) of Wicken was acquired by the National Trust for £10,000 in May 1899 – but, since then, 54 separate acquisitions have taken the total in its ownership to 324 hectares (800 acres).

Today it offers 29 kilometres (18 miles) of walks – including an all-weather boardwalk – a demonstration garden, fields of litter (a diverse, tall grass vegetation), ponds, dykes and a milk parsley field (parts of which are cut each year to encourage Swallowtail butterfly caterpillars).

There is also a sedge field with peat workings, Lode Bank (a good place for butterflies), Wicken Lode (home to Britain's largest dragonfly) and Adventurer's Fen (an important area for birds).

Facilities include an education area, a residential base camp for conservation volunteers, education groups and training courses, a picnic site, shop and the William Thorpe visitor centre.

This was named after a professor who prevented Adventurer's Fen from being drained and used as a bombing range in the Second World War.

Wicken Fen is open from dawn to dusk every day except Christmas Day but some paths may be closed in very wet weather.

The Visitor Centre, where hot and cold drinks, ice creams and sweets are available, is normally open daily between 10am and 5pm from Tuesday to Sunday each week, except on Christmas Day – but may occasionally close during Winter.

The Fen Cottage and Garden is open between 2pm and 5pm on Sundays and Bank Holidays from April to October and also on some other days in the Summer.

A tower hide and six other hides are available, together with guided walks, dozens of special events and children's days which are held throughout the year.

Dogs are welcome on the reserve but must be kept on a short lead at all times. There is a nearby area where they can run free.

Wicken Corn Windmill

This 1813 smock mill would originally have had cloth sails, rather than the shuttered type it bears today.

Currently nearing full restoration by a specially-formed Preservation Group, it is open at various times throughout the year (please phone for details).

Willers Mill Wildlife Park

This wildlife centre at Shepreth, south-west of Cambridge, started life as a refuge for injured and orphaned birds and mammals.

Today the park, which is set in natural grounds and lakes and open to the public daily, is home to a famous collection of animals and birds as well as a fish farm.

There is a children's play area and cafeteria and a recent addition is the Water World and Bug City feature which houses fish and insects – including leaf cutter ants – from around the world.

Wimpole Hall

This National Trust-owned property at Arrington, 13 kilometres (eight miles) south west of Cambridge, was built mainly in the 18th century.

It is surrounded by 142 hectares (350 acres) of parkland landscaped by Charles Bridgeman, Capability Brown and Humphrey Repton.

Wimpole features several different trails which members of the public can follow around the Estate.

Other attractions include:

The Chinese Bridge – a wooden construction originally designed by Lancelot Brown.

The folly – a Gothic Tower built on Johnson's Hill in 1774 to look like a medieval ruin which suggested the place was ancient and the family went back to the dawn of time.

Wimpole Home Farm has a collection of farm machinery and many rare breeds of animals.

The Hall and Gardens are open between 1pm and 5pm from mid-March to the end of July and from the beginning of September to the end of October daily (excluding Mondays and Fridays except Good Friday and Bank Holiday Mondays, when open 11am–5pm) plus the whole of August (closed Mondays except Bank Holiday Monday).

The Farm is open between 10.30am and 5pm daily from mid-March to early November (excluding Mondays and Fridays except Good Friday and Bank Holiday Mondays).

Wimpole's licensed **Old Rectory restaurant** is open between 11am and 5.30pm from mid-March to the end of October on the same days as the Hall and between 11am and 4pm

Linton Zoo
Tel./Fax. 01223 891308

**Milton Country Park
(ranger service)**
Tel. 01223 443000

Wicken Fen
Tel./Fax. 01353 720274
e-mail: awndjc@
smtp.ntrust.org.uk
web: www.wicken.org.uk

Wicken Windmill
Tel. 01664 822751
web:
www.wickenmill.fsnet.co.uk

Willers Mill Wildlife Park
Tel. 01763 262226
Fax. 01763 260582

**Wimpole Hall and Wimpole
Home Farm**
Tel. 01223 207257
Fax. 01223 207838
e-mail: aweusr@
smtp.ntrust.org.uk
web: www.wimpole.org

**Wimpole Hall Old Rectory
restaurant**
Tel. 01223 208670

from the beginning of November to December 23rd.

National Trust restaurants try to recreate traditional and regional Victorian dishes where possible – rather than serve up modern dishes.

Wimpole Hall

Essex and Suffolk Borders

An area of outstanding natural beauty extending inland from the coast at the mouth of the Stour to Colchester via the charming and world-famous Dedham Vale.

This part of the country is also rich in historical associations, which have continued over the centuries.

In the days of the Romans there was the Emperor Claudius, whose Great Temple was at Colchester while, in more modern times, the area gave birth to the talents of the celebrated landscape artist John Constable.

i Tourist Information Centres

Colchester
Tel. 01206 282920; Fax. 01206 282924

Flatford (April to September)
Tel. 01206 299460

Non-funded Tourist Information Point
Manningtree
Tel. 01206 396170

Ordnance Survey Maps
OS Landranger sheet numbers: 168, 169

Willy Lott's Cottage, Flatford

Colchester

Britain's oldest town boasts a 2000-year history which, apart from the Romans, also includes links with Saxons and Normans.

The walls were built by the Romans, using alternate courses of stone and tile on the outer faces, between 65 and 80 AD.

In **Layer Marney Tower,** which stands among grounds containing deer and rare breeds, Colchester has the tallest Tudor gate tower in England, with exquisite 16th century Italianate decoration.

The town also claims a number of historic churches and chapels, including Britain's earliest-known Christian church.

The castle, in the High Street, features the largest keep ever built by the Normans.

It was constructed between 1076 and 1125 – over the top of the Great Temple of Claudius, built by the Romans 1000 years earlier.

Now a museum (open 10am to 5pm from Monday to Saturday all year round and 1pm to 5pm on Sunday as well from March to November only), it houses one of the finest collections of Roman archaeology in the country.

There are many 'hands on' displays and visitors can delve into Colchester's murkier past by touring the prisons.

The adjacent and award-winning Castle Park is a Victorian horticultural oasis right in the town centre, covering 13.5 gently sloping hectares (33 acres).

It includes formal gardens, a sensory garden, children's boating lake and playground, toy and costume museum and Victorian bandstand.

Museums in the town include the High Street **Natural History Museum** (open March to November), which offers a 'hands-on' perspective to the local natural environment from the Ice Age to the present.

Meanwhile **Tymperley's Clock Museum** (open Tuesday to Saturday between 10am and 5pm from April to October only) is in a beautiful Grade

Colchester Castle

II listed 15th century timber-framed house in Trinity Street.

Other places worth a visit include **The Mercury** – the town's repertory theatre, which offers a broad spectrum of performances for all age groups and houses an art gallery, studio theatre, café, bar and restaurant.

For families with youngsters, good bets are two Cowdray Centre attractions – **Go Bananas** (open daily), a 12,000-foot warehouse converted into a three storey play area for youngsters and **Leisure World,** which features a leisure pool, flume rides, spa pools and water cannons as well as a wide range of sports activities.

Colchester Area

Bourne Mill

Built as a fishing lodge on the banks of Bourne Brook 1.6 kilometres (one mile) south of Colchester town centre in 1591, this building features 'stepped' Dutch gables.

It was converted in the 19th century into a mill for yarn spinning and later flour milling and much of the original machinery, including the waterwheel, is intact and still working.

The National Trust property can be visited between 2pm and 5.30pm on Sundays and Tuesdays from June to August as well as Bank Holiday Sundays and Mondays throughout the year.

Coggeshall Heritage Centre

Heritage museum at St Peter's Hall, Stoneham Street, displaying items of local interest, supplemented by exhibitions on a theme relating to the past of this historic wool town.

Colchester Zoo

This award-winning attraction, at Maldon Road, Stanway, on the outskirts of Colchester, is one of the best zoos in Europe and home to some 200 different species of animals from around the world.

Recent new enclosures include Penguin Shores, Wilds of Asia (lion-tailed macaques, red pandas, Asian fishing cats and reptiles), Edge of Africa (cheetah, spotted hyena, primates and wild dogs), Serengeti Plains (lions) and Spirit of Africa (elephants).

The free Tanganyika Road Train takes visitors around lemur island

☎ FAX 💻

Layer Marney Tower
Tel. 01206 330784

Colchester Castle Museum
Tel. 01206 282931/2

Natural History Museum
Tel. 01206 282931

Tymperley's Clock Museum
Tel. 01206 282943

Mercury Theatre
(Box office)
Tel. 01206 573948

Go Bananas
Tel. 01206 761762

Colchester Leisure World
Tel. 01206 282000

Bourne Mill
Tel. 01206 572422

Coggeshall Heritage Centre
Tel. 01376 563003
e-mail:
spratcliffe@btinternet.com
web: www.btinternet.com/
~coggeshall

Colchester Zoo
Tel. 01206 331292
Fax. 01206 331392
e-mail: colchester.zoo@
btinternet.com
web: www.colchester-zoo.co.uk

Grange Barn, Coggeshall

and a train ride runs on the hour or constantly at busy times.

Colchester Zoo is open daily, except on Christmas Day, from 9.30am with last admissions at 5.30pm in the summer and one hour before dusk during off season.

Facilities are available for the disabled but the hilly terrain can be hard going for wheelchairs and pushchairs. Because of this an easier route, maps of which can be picked up on arrival, has been developed.

No dogs or pets are allowed.

Colne Valley Railway

Based at Castle Hedingham, south west of Sudbury, this steam railway houses the largest collection of operational heritage engines, carriages and wagons in the county.

It also runs through one of the prettiest parts of the Colne Valley and visitors can picnic on a large grassland area beside the river.

The railway is open between 10am and 5pm from the beginning of March until December 23rd (closed December 24th to January 1st).

East Anglian Railway Museum

The museum – at Chappel Station, seven miles west of Colchester –

Colne Valley Railway
Tel. 01787 461174
Fax. 01787 462254
web: www.cvr.org.uk

East Anglian Railway Museum
Tel. 01206 242524

Grange Barn
Tel. 01376 562226

Hedingham Castle
Tel. 01787 460261
Fax. 01787 461473
e-mail: hedinghamcastle@
aspects.net

Marks Hall Estate
Tel. 01376 563084
Fax. 01376 563132

Paycocke's House
Tel. 01376 561305

spans 150 years of railway history.

It is open daily between 10am and 5pm throughout the year with the exception of Christmas Day and Boxing Day.

Grange Barn, Coggeshall

The oldest-surviving timber framed barn in Europe was built as part of the Cistercian Monastery of Coggeshall and dates back to around 1140 AD.

Inside the building – which is open between 1pm and 5pm on Tuesdays, Thursdays, Sundays and Bank Holiday Mondays from the beginning of April until the middle of October – are displays of barn restoration, together with a collection of farm carts and wagons.

Hedingham Castle

The castle consists of a splendid Norman keep built in 1140 by the famous de Veres, Earls of Oxford.

Hedingham, which was visited by Henry VIII and Queen Elizabeth I and besieged by King John, features a banqueting hall with minstrels' gallery and the finest Norman arch in England.

Around it there are attractive grounds with peaceful woodland and lakeside walks, making the site ideal for family picnics.

The castle is open between 10am

Paycocke's House, Coggeshall

and 5pm daily from the week before Easter to the end of October.

Marks Hall Estate

Ancient woodlands form a backdrop to this historic estate which features a new arboretum and a programme of events (call for details).

The estate includes ornamental lakes, cascades, a walled garden, parkland and mature avenues.

Paycocke's House

This delightful merchant's house, in the attractive town of Coggeshall, dates from around 1500 and features unusually rich panelling and woodcarvings.

Inside the building there is a display of Coggeshall lace and outside there is a pleasant garden.

The National Trust property is open between 2pm and 5.30pm on Tuesdays, Thursdays and Bank Holiday Mondays from the beginning of April to mid-October.

Constable Country

The beautiful and inspiring area given this name is centred on the hamlet of Flatford and the villages of Dedham and East Bergholt.

The locality is a magnet for tourists from all over the world through the paintings of John Constable (1776–1837), who immortalised the landscape of gentle hills, valleys, rivers and streams.

Constable, who was born in East Bergholt and went to school in Dedham, wrote of the area: "I love every stile and stump and lane... these scenes made me a painter."

Dedham vale is a rich mosaic of lowland landscape and wildlife habitat. Moorhen, coot and ducks thrive among the willow, hemlock and yellow cress along the river and the banks are home to many diverse species of water plant and animal life.

Both East Bergholt and Dedham have been settled since at least

Saxon times and Flatford boasts 'The Swannes Nest', which may have been a fortified area built to repel the Vikings or an early church.

Bridge Cottage, Flatford

A 16th century thatched complex, which is run by the National Trust and includes a Constable exhibition.

Hour-long **guided walks** to the sites of Constable's paintings can be booked here and usually start at 11am, 1pm and 2.30pm (but sometimes more frequently) in the first two weeks of April and then continue from May onwards.

It is best to phone for times and availability, especially during the second two weeks of April as walks are led by volunteers.

Pre-booking is available for groups and audio tapes may be hired when guided walks are not available.

There is also a restored dry dock, shop and tea room – where the National Trust tries to include recipes relevant to the history of its buildings and often holds special events.

Flatford's **tearooms** are open between 11am and 5.30pm from Wednesday to Sunday included in March, April and October.

From May to the end of September the hours are from 10am to 5.30pm daily and from November to December 19th 11am to 3.30pm from Wednesday to Sunday.

Parking for Flatford is at a private car park in the village and there is a Visitor Information Centre, which has toilets – including those for people with disabilities – a baby changing area and parking for disabled visitors.

Further details of Constable Country are available from Colchester Visitor Centre at 1 Queen Street, Colchester, Essex CO1 2PG and Flatford Visitor Information Centre is at Flatford Lane, Flatford, East Bergholt, Essex CO7 6UL.

Carters Vineyards

A two-hectare (5-acre) vineyard set in eight times that area of conservation countryside at Boxted just west of Flatford and Dedham.

Flatford Mill

A vineyard trail leads into a nature ramble around lakes, wildflower meadows and new woodlands.

The vineyard – which includes a winery powered by electricity from solar cells and a wind generator – is open between 11am and 5pm from Easter to the end of September. There is also a restored dry dock, tearooms – where special events are often held – and shop.

Dedham Art & Craft Centre and Toy Museum

Housed in a converted church, the centre has three floors of arts, crafts and studio workshops as well as a toy museum and restaurant.

It is open between 10am and 5pm daily from April to December and from Tuesday to Sunday only for the remaining three months.

Dedham Vale Family Farm

Rare breeds of British farm animals and a petting paddock where children can stroke the animals.

The farm, which includes a children's playground, picnic area and shop, is open between 10am and 5pm daily from the beginning of March to the middle of September.

Field Studies Council

This Flatford Mill centre offers a wide-ranging programme of residential and day courses in landscape, wildlife, plant life, portrait and still life painting plus courses covering walking, writing, calligraphy and

Bridge Cottage
Tel. 01206 298260
Fax. 01206 299193
e-mail: afdckx@
smtp.ntrust.org.uk

Constable Walk
Tel. 01206 298260

Flatford Tearooms
Tel. 01206 298260/ 298865
Fax. 01206 299193
e-mail: afdckx@
smtp.ntrust.org.uk

Carters Vineyards
Tel. 01206 271136

Dedham Art & Craft Centre and Toy Museum
Tel. 01206 322666

Dedham Vale Family Farm
Tel. 01206 323111

Flatford Field Studies Council
Tel. 01206 298283
Fax. 01206 298892
e-mail: fsc.flatford@
ukonline.co.uk

Stour Trusty II
Tel. 01206 393680

River Stour Trust (secretary)
Tel. 01268 753245

medieval houses.

A guide to subjects is available and accommodation options include the 18th century Mill, Willy Lott's Cottage or a medieval hall house at Valley Farm.

Flatford Boat Trip

The Stour Trusty II is operated by the **River Stour Trust,** established as a registered charity in 1968 to protect and enhance public navigation rights and access to one of the longest and most beautiful rivers in East Anglia.

The Edwardian-style 12-seater electric boat runs 30-minute trips from Flatford to Fen Bridge (half way to Dedham), from Easter to the beginning of October.

It operates between 11am and 5pm on Sundays and Bank Holidays with Wednesday trips also available during school holidays.

Stour Trusty II is the only powered craft allowed on this stretch of the river and aims to encourage people to leave their cars at home and use other means of getting to Flatford and Dedham.

For details of Stour Trusty II trips and charters, contact David Nicholls at Portmark House, 55/57 High Street, Manningtree, Essex CO11 1AH.

Gibbonsgate Field, Flatford

A circular walk of just under 1.6 kilometres (one mile) with a picnic area, views over Cattawade Marshes – a Site of Specific Scientific Interest for its bird life – and a bird hide overlooking Gibbonsgate Lake, which is open to the public.

The entrance to the field is just alongside Willy Lott's House.

Museum of Rural Bygones, Flatford

The museum is housed in premises which were built in 1740 as a granary and later became a steam mill.

It was opened in 1986 to reflect the clothing, tools and transport of Constable's era but has since grown into an Aladdin's Cave of later bygones guaranteed to stir the memories of older visitors.

The collection includes 150 steam irons, 20 early bicycles, and some very early washing machines.

The museum is open from 10am to dusk throughout the summer months.

St Mary the Virgin Church, East Bergholt

Nayland

Constable's painting, Christ Blessing the Bread and Wine, still hangs in the village church.

Rowing

Rowing boats can be hired at both Dedham and Flatford.

Maestrani Boatyard at Dedham is opposite the water mill – the turning to the yard is between the bridge and The Mallard Tearooms.

Tripp Boatyard at Flatford is beside the bridge and boats are normally available from early morning until late evening, throughout the year, depending on demand.

Sir Alfred Munnings Art Museum

At Castle House, Dedham has a museum filled with the works of Sir Alfred Munnings (b. 1878), who lived there from 1919 until his death in 1959.

Munnings – who achieved fame for his racehorse and equestrian paintings, although many consider his earlier pictures of rural life were better – called it "the house of my dreams."

Castle House is a mixture of Tudor and Georgian periods and retains its essential character through the retention of Munnings' original furniture.

The museum – which is roughly a kilometre (three-quarters of a mile) from the village centre, at the corner of East Lane and Castle Hill – adds special exhibitions to its permanent collection each year.

Opening times are between 2pm and 5pm every Sunday, Wednesday and Bank Holiday Monday from Easter Sunday to the first Sunday in October and between the same times on Thursdays and Saturdays in August only.

St Mary the Virgin Church, Dedham

This building, in the High Street, will be familiar to many – since it is featured in several of Constable's paintings.

St Mary the Virgin Church, East Bergholt

This striking church contains both the tomb of Constable's parents – in its north east corner (the artist himself was buried in Hampstead cemetery) – and the grave of Willy Lott (by the main path next to the East end of the Lady Chapel).

Its churchyard also features a 16th century bellcage constructed as a temporary measure in 1531 – to house the bells for the church tower, which was never actually built.

Assistance with the bell tower costs was promised by Cardinal Wolsey – but his downfall cut short the possibility of help from this source and work ceased.

Although other bell cages exist elsewhere, this is the only place where ringing is by force of hand applied directly to the bells – the heaviest five bells tolled anywhere in England – and not via rope and wheel.

Ringing takes place every Sunday between 9.30am and 10am throughout the year as well as, in Summer only, between 6pm and 6.30pm on the evening of the same day and Thursday evenings (for practice) plus, as required, for weddings.

Manningtree

Although the origins of its name are obscure, it is known that England's smallest town was the home of the Manni tribe, who greeted Caesar in 55 BC.

Also recorded is the fact that it had become a thriving port known as Manytre by Tudor times.

Much of the wealth in Elizabethan times came from the cloth trade and fine examples of weavers' cottages remain in Brook Street and South Street.

One of the most famous people connected with Manningtree, unhappily, is Matthew Hopkins - the notorious 17th century Witchfinder General, who is buried at Mistley Heath.

Essex Secret Bunker

Manningtree Museum

The museum holds permanent items and photographs concerning the heritage of Manningtree, Mistley and Lawford and also aims to stage two special exhibitions each year.

Based at the High Street library, it is open between 10am and 12 noon plus 2 and 6pm on Fridays and 10am and 12 noon on Saturdays.

Manningtree Area

Alton Water

Alton Water, which is owned by Anglian Water, is at Stutton, about eight kilometres (five miles) north-east of Manningtree and was opened to the public in 1982.

Today it is a top centre for watersports and about 100,000 visitors go there for fishing, windsurfing, cycling, walking and aqua golf each year.

A visitor centre displays the history of the reservoir and features a spacious cafeteria (open daily except on Mondays) with panoramic views.

The top end of the reservoir has been set aside as a wildlife sanctuary and several conservation projects have been introduced in conjunction with Suffolk Wildlife Trust.

These include construction of a new bird hide and viewing platform, islands and rafts for nesting birds and a shallow lagoon area for wading birds and wildfowl.

Bikes for rides round the reservoir can be obtained from Alton Water Cycle Hire, at the southern end, every week-end as well as on Bank Holidays and in school holidays.

Alton Water itself is open all year

round between at least 10am and 4pm.

Essex Secret Bunker

The underground former county nuclear headquarters in Shrublands Road, Mistley, near Manningtree, reveals the secrets of the 'Cold War' through displays, cinemas and sound effects.

The bunker is open daily between 10.30am and 5pm (6pm in August) from the beginning of April to the end of September and between 10.30am and 4.30pm on Saturdays and Sundays for the rest of the year (closed December 20th to January 5th).

HMS Ganges Association Museum

The museum, at Shotley Marina, has photographs and artefacts connected with this famous boys' naval training establishment and is open from between 11am and 5pm on Saturdays, Sundays and Bank Holidays from April to October.

Manningtree to Flatford Walk

The Dedham Vale and Stour Valley Countryside Project has a remit for landscape and conservation and is promoting informal recreation in the whole of the Stour Valley.

At certain times of the year, Flatford Mill becomes highly congested with traffic.

So the Countryside Project, along with the National Trust, is trying to encourage people to use more environmentally-friendly means of transport, such as train and bicycle - or foot!

Manningtree is accessible from many mainline stations, including Colchester, Ipswich, Norwich and London Liverpool Street.

The walk from there to Flatford is well signed, particularly picturesque and takes only around half an hour.

Along the way there is a variety of things to see including Cattawade Marshes, reed beds, the tidal River Stour and Flatford Mill.

In March some of the bush-lined lanes are full of Spring Beauty, a

plant which was carried in on the grain barges from Manningtree.

Mistley Place Park

A menagerie of rescued animals and birds roaming freely at Mistley Place Park – 10 hectares (25 acres) of countryside overlooking the Stour Valley 16 kilometres (10 miles) north-east of Colchester.

Mistley is open daily between 10am and 6pm (or dusk if earlier) all year round.

Pin Mill

A woodland area along the southern banks of the Orwell estuary near the village of Chelmondiston.

It is accessible only on foot but there are fine views of the river with its collection of Thames barges and pleasure craft and a circular walk leads through both woodland and newly-created heathland.

Museum of Rural Bygones
Tel. 01206 298111

Maestrani Boatyard
Tel. 01206 323153

Flatford Boat Hire
(Derek Tripp)
Tel. 01206 298111

Sir Alfred Munnings
Art Museum
Tel./Fax. 01206 322127

Manningtree Museum
Tel. 01206 395548

Alton Water
Visitor Centre, cafeteria &
cycle hire
Tel. 01473 328873
fishery
Tel. 01473 589105
Watersports Centre
Tel. 01473 328408

Essex Secret Bunker
Tel. 01206 392271

HMS Ganges Association
Museum
Tel. 01473 684749/ 311322/
787291

Mistley Place Park
Tel. 01206 396483

East Essex

A county which shows a range of faces to the world – from the teeming Summer resorts of Clacton and Southend to the tranquillity of the Blackwater Estuary.

Both Clacton and Southend boast their own piers which, with the addition of the one at Walton, must give Essex one of the greatest lengths, if not highest counts, of these popular Victorian constructions in the country.

The county is also known for its yachting centres, such as Brightlingsea, Burnham-on-Crouch and Titchmarsh as well as the port of Maldon – home of the last of the hundreds of sailing barges which used to ply their trade along the Essex and Kent coasts.

It's an area steeped in earlier history, too, taking in Stone Age settlements as well as the scenes of a bloody battle between the Saxons and Vikings and the massacre of the leaders of the Peasants' Revolt.

Tourist Information Centres

Burnham-on-Crouch
Tel. 01621 786376; Fax. 01621 784962
e-mail: bvda@freenet.co.uk

Chelmsford
Tel. 01245 283400; Fax. 01245 430705

Clacton-on-Sea
Tel. 01255 423400; Fax. 01255 430906

Harwich
Tel. 01255 506139; Fax. 01255 240570

Maldon
Tel. 01621 856503; Fax. 01621 875873
e-mail: tic@maldon.gov.uk

Southend-on-Sea
Tel. 01702 215120; Fax. 01702 431449

Walton-on-the-Naze
(for Frinton-on-Sea)
Tel. 01255 675542

Ordnance Survey Maps
OS Landranger sheet numbers: 167, 168

The Blackwater Estuary

Maldon

In AD 991, the invading Vikings attacked the Saxons at Maldon.

Both sides suffered great losses and Byrhtnoth, the Saxon leader, died in the battle. Yet, his heroic defence saved the town from occupation.

Today, there is a much friendlier welcome awaiting visitors to Maldon and the many attractions around the town which the Saxons knew as Maeldune.

All Saints Church

The church at the top of the High Street has an unusual 12th century triangular tower and monuments which reflect some of the past residents of the area – including the Saxon warrior Byrhtnoth and Sir Robert D'Arcy.

There is also a window dedicated to the Reverend Lawrence Washington, who was rector at another All Saints (that of nearby Purleigh) from 1632 to 1643.

For Lawrence's two sons emigrated to America and he was the great-great-grandfather of the first president of the USA.

Maeldune Heritage Centre

The Maeldune (meaning: 'Cross or monument on a hilltop') Heritage Centre harks back to an age when the fate of Anglo-Saxon England depended on keeping the Scandinavian invaders at bay.

Most notably, it houses the famous Maldon Embroidery – a 12.8m (42-ft) long work, which recalls the Battle and took 80 local women to complete.

The centre is open between 1pm and 4.30pm Monday to Saturday from April to September and between noon and 3pm Thursday to Saturday from October to March.

Moot Hall

The word 'Moot' is Anglo-Saxon for 'meeting place' – and the Corporation of Maldon purchased this building for that purpose in 1576 for the sum of £55.

Visits and tours of the Moot Hall – which includes an interesting 19th century 'Dickensian' courtroom – can be made by appointment with the Town Council.

Museums

Maldon and District Agricultural and Domestic Museum features ancient tractors, motorbikes, mangles and a host of pieces – some going back to the 18th century.

Maldon District Museum concentrates on the social history of the town from 1810 to 1950.

Plume Library

The Plume Library on Market Hill, in the same building as the Maeldune Heritage Centre, is the second oldest library in Britain.

Its books are too precious to lend out but the collection is still in the Library Room built for it 300 years ago.

Thomas Plume was Archdeacon of Rochester and his massive collection of books ran to 7000 – ranging in date from 1487 to 1704 – by the time he died.

St Mary's Church

St Mary's Church, a prominent feature on the town's skyline, was much more than a church. It was also a lighthouse.

In olden days, a beacon shone out from the tower to guide sailors into harbour.

Maldon Area

Blackwater Estuary

The Blackwater is one of the most unspoiled UK habitats for wildlife, especially wintering birds, and avocet, godwit and redshank are often seen here.

The estuary, reputedly the saltiest in Britain, is especially important because it lies beneath a migratory route used by a large number of bird species – at least 11 of which use it for food and roosting.

The Blackwater National Nature

Maldon quay side

Maeldune Heritage Centre
Tel. 01621 851628

Moot Hall
Tel. 01621 857373

Maldon and District Agricultural and Domestic Museum
Tel. 01621 788647

Maldon District Museum
Tel. 01621 842688

Plume Library
Tel. 01621 854051

Bradwell Shell Bank
Tel. 01277 354034

Reserve consists of the RSPB Old Hall Marshes Reserve and the mudflats around Tollesbury Wick.

Both are visible from the sea wall footpaths but a permit (obtainable only in advance from the RSPB Old Hall Marshes reserve – Tel. 01621 869015) is required to explore the riches of Old Hall, which represents the largest block of grazing marsh in Essex. It is open daily except Tuesdays.

Visitors can also pick up a copy of the North Blackwater Trail from the local tourist centre.

Bradwell Shell Bank

The Dengie Peninsula lies between the rivers Blackwater and Crouch and several parts of the area are designated Sites of Special Scientific Interest.

Located in the north-eastern corner of the peninsula is the Bradwell Shell Bank, one of the remotest wildlife areas, where there is a 10-kilometre (6½-mile) walk.

As well as all the natural features,

Northey Island and causeway

the walk also passes a World War II airfield, **Bradwell Nuclear Power Station** (open between 10am and 4pm daily, March to October), and **St Peter's-on-the-Wall** (654 AD).

Burnham-on-Crouch

Burnham is a quiet, unspoilt riverside town with a distinctly nautical air – especially during 'Burnham Week' (August Bank Holiday).

The town is sometimes called 'the Cowes of the East Coast', primarily because it is headquarters for the Burnham Sailing Club, Burnham Yacht Harbour, Crouch Yacht Club,

Bradwell Power Station
Tel. 01621 873395

St Peter's-on-the-Wall
Tel. 01621 776203

Lady Essex II ferry and tour service
Tel. 01702 258600 or 258870

Blackwater Boats
Tel. 01206 853282

Chelmer Boats
Tel. 01245 225520

Burnham Museum
Tel. 01621 783444

Mangapps Farm Railway Museum
Tel. 01621 784898

Mersea Island Museum
Tel. 01206 385191

Museum of Power
Tel. 01621 843183

New Hall Vineyards
Tel. 01621 828343

Northey Island (Warden)
Tel. 01621 853142

Royal Burnham Yacht Club – which mounted the 1983 British challenge for the America's Cup – and the Royal Corinthian Yacht Club.

The Lady Essex II operates ferry services between here and Wallasea and other cruises.

Chelmer and Blackwater Navigation

An important link between Maldon – at the head of the Blackwater and Chelmer rivers – and the County Town of Chelmsford, is the Chelmer and Blackwater Navigation.

The canal, which was completed in 1797, runs for 22 kilometres (14 miles) through some of the county's most beautiful rural countryside and drops 24 metres (77ft) through 13 locks.

Narrow boats are available for hire from **Blackwater Boats** and **Chelmer Cruises.**

Maldon Salt Works

Maldon – where it is said the sea is at its most saline – is famed for its salt works, established in 1777.

It is the only place in the country producing crystalline salt from seawater, continuing a tradition of salt-making around the estuary that goes back to Iron Age times some 4000 years ago.

In 1790 a saline bath was built close to the salt works to take advantage of the growing popularity of salt-water bathing.

Museums

Burnham Museum concentrates on maritime, agricultural and social history.

Maldon Salt Works

Mangapps Farm Railway Museum, near Burnham, includes a collection of railway relics; steam and diesel locomotives, carriages and wagons, historic railway buildings and signalling equipment.

It has a complete country station, with rides behind a steam or vintage diesel loco, a one kilometre (¾ mile) length of railway track, picnic areas and a shop.

Mersea Island Museum is open during the Summer months and features collections focusing on the history of the island.

The Museum of Power, at the Steam Pumping Station at Langford, near Maldon includes steam traction engines.

New Hall Vineyards

The nine hectare (20-acre) vineyards at Purleigh near Maldon were established by the Greenwood family in 1969 and have become the largest of their kind in East Anglia.

The company offers wine tastings and guided tours as well as hosting an annual English Wine Festival.

New Hall is open between 10am and 5pm from Monday to Friday and 10am to 1.30pm on Saturdays and Sundays.

Northey Island

The causeway linking Maldon with Northey Island was the key location for the Battle of Maldon (AD 991).

More peaceful today, the island extends to 121 hectares (300 acres), including 97 hectares (240 acres) of saltings subject to tidal flood.

Northey, which includes a nature reserve, belongs to the National Trust and is designated a Site of Special Scientific Interest.

The island has become a prime habitat for a number of bird species, particularly Brent geese.

The causeway access can only be used at low water. So local tide tables should be consulted before planning a trip across.

Anyone interested in visiting the island will also need to obtain a permit from the warden at least 24 hours in advance.

Thames Barges

Thames sailing barges, with their characteristic tan sails and spritsail rig, have a long history on the Essex and Kent coasts – and they feature in the traditional race at Maldon each June.

In the early 1900s there were some 2000 Thames barges at work. Shallow drafts gave them access to the muddy creeks and inlets of the inland ports and farms.

They fell out of use with the development of road transport but some were later fitted with auxiliary engines and others became houseboats.

Tiptree Preserves

Strawberries, plums, cherries, greengages, quinces, medlars and loganberries.

All feature in the 25–30 million jars of preserves manufactured each year by **Wilkin & Sons,** whose headquarters are at Tiptree, north east of Maldon.

The company, founded by Arthur Charles Wilkin in 1885, farms 404 hectares (1000 acres) of land at Tiptree, Tollesbury and Goldhanger.

As well as the more familiar fruits listed above, the farm also produces the only commercially-grown 'little scarlet' wild strawberry – almost certainly introduced from North America and first cultivated at Tiptree late in the 19th century.

Tiptree, which features a shop, tearoom and village and jam-making museum (free admission), is open between 10am and 5pm from Monday to Saturday and 12 noon to 5pm on Sundays in June, July and August.

Braintree

This small market town is set at the heart of what was one of the main textile centres of Europe.

In fact, in South Street, it boasts the country's last remaining hand loom **silk weavers,** who can be seen at work on 150-year-old looms.

Visitors can discover how silk fabric is produced from the raw material right through to the finished cloth.

There is also a permanent 'Threads of Time' display, relating to the local textile heritage, at Braintree's **museum** and exhibition centre in Manor Street.

Additionally this centre features a Victorian classroom, a small apothecary's garden, a craft shop and natural history gallery.

Today, an abundance of antiques shops can be found in Braintree and the surrounding area – perhaps not surprisingly, as much of the popular 'Lovejoy' television series was shot here.

Braintree Area

Bocking Windmill

An early 18th century postmill – complete, both externally and internally – and a small collection of historic agricultural items.

Boydells Dairy Farm

A family run dairy farm at Weathersfield, specialising in milking sheep, also goats and cows, but featuring many other farm animals.

Everything is explained and there is fun and education for all – including children, for whom there are goat and donkey cart rides.

Cressing Temple Barns

An ancient moated farmstead with a fascinating range of rural buildings and two vast oak barns built with outstanding craftsmanship some 800 years ago for the Knights Templar.

The site features a new exhibition, plus a delightful walled garden in the Tudor style.

Felsted Vineyards

This 4.9 hectare (12-acre) vineyard set in the Essex countryside at Crix Green, Felstead, offers guided tours and tutored tastings for groups of between 12 and 50 people.

But there is also free entry for casual visitors, who may stroll

Wilkin & Sons Limited
Tel. 01621 815407
Fax. 01621 814555
e-mail: tiptree@tiptree.com
web: www.tiptree.com

Working Silk Museum
Tel. 01376 553393
Fax. 01376 330642
web: www. humphriesweaving.co.uk

Braintree District Museum
Tel. 01376 325266
Fax. 01376 344345
e-mail: jean@ bdcmuseum.demon.co.uk

Bocking Windmill
Tel. 01376 324660

Boydells Dairy Farm
Tel. 01371 850481
e-mail: boydells@farmline.com
web: www.members.farmline.com/ boydells

Cressing Temple
Tel. 01376 584903
e-mail: cressing.temple@ essexcc.gov.uk

Felsted Vineyards
Tel. 01245 361504
Fax. 01245 361504
e-mail: felsted.vineyards@virgin.net

Thames barge on the Blackwater

Ridley's Brewery
Tel. 01371 820316
e-mail:
insight@ridleys.co.uk
web: www.ridleys.co.uk

Chelmsford Cathedral
Tel. 01245 294480

**Chelmsford and Essex Museum/
Essex Regimental Museum**
Tel. 01245 353066

Dorothy L Sayers Centre
Tel. 01376 519625
Fax. 01376 501913
e-mail:
centre@sayers.org.uk

Hylands House
Tel. 01245 355455
e-mail: mailbox@
chelmsfordbc.gov.uk

**Marsh Farm and
Country Park**
Tel. 01245 324191 or
321552

town – with a famous market of more than a hundred stalls – remains the centre of Essex social, cultural, sporting and economic life.

Chelmsford Cathedral Festival

The annual Cathedral Festival in May includes concerts, talks, exhibitions and other fringe events involving the whole community.

The building itself, which dates back to 1420, is open between 8.15am and 6pm from Monday to Saturday and between 7.30am and 12.30pm and 2pm to 7pm on Sundays.

Museums

The Chelmsford and Essex Museum includes displays of social history and archaeology and the 'Story of Chelmsford' exhibition, which follows the area's fortunes from the Ice Age to today.

The museum is open all year between 10am and 5pm from Monday to Saturday and Bank Holidays as well as 2–5pm on Sundays.

The Essex Regiment Museum, adjoining the general museum and open at the same times, tells the story of the 250-year-old regiment through mess silver, uniforms, medals, drums, letters and diaries.

Visiting The Essex Police Museum is by appointment only. Write to the museum c/o Essex Police Headquarters, PO Box No. 2 Springfield, Chelmsford CM2 6DA.

Hylands House

Chelmsford Area

Dorothy L. Sayers Centre

A reference collection at Newland Street, Witham, of books by and about Dorothy L Sayers, novelist, theologian and Dante scholar, who lived in Witham for many years.

Hylands House and Park

The grounds of Hylands House are home to the Chelmsford Spectacular – an award-winning open-air music and entertainment festival enjoyed by up to 65,000 visitors each year.

The exteriors of the partially-restored Grade II listed Georgian mansion – which was designed by Humphrey Repton for Sir John Comyns – have been restored to an 1820–30 period by the council and work is now under way to restore the interiors to their former glory.

Hylands House, which stands in more than 202 hectares (500 acres) of parkland, is open Sundays and Mondays throughout the year and often features other events, including art exhibitions, concerts and nature walks.

Marsh Farm Country Park

Close to South Woodham Ferrers, this is a working farm and country park on the River Crouch.

Marsh Farm is open daily between 10am and 4.30pm from mid-February to the end of October; 10am and 5.30pm at weekends, on Bank Holidays and in Summer time; and 10am and 5.30pm at weekends only from early November to mid-December.

through the vineyard and taste the wines.

Teas are available and light lunches are served at weekends.

Ridley's Brewery

Built originally in the 19th century, the brewery at Hartford End, Felstead, still uses the same building and methods to produce a range of traditional cask conditioned beers.

Chelmsford

Chelmsford was an important Roman crossroads called *Caesaromagus* (Caesar's market place).

Guglielmo Marconi (1874–1937), the father of wireless, had a factory in Chelmsford and Dame Nellie Melba made her famous pioneering radio recital there in 1920.

Charles Dickens and the Duke of Wellington drank at the local Black Boy Inn and Oliver Goldsmith had a house in town.

Eight hundred years on, the county

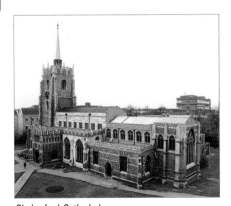
Chelmsford Cathedral

Moulsham Mill

This riverside mill has been a city centre landmark for more than a hundred years.

It produced flour until 1963 but now houses a variety of artistic workshops which are open between 9am and 5.30pm from Monday to Friday and 9am to 5pm on Saturdays.

Royal Horticultural Society Garden – Hyde Hall

A national collection of viburnum is one of the specialities of this garden at Rettendon, near Chelmsford.

It is a three-hectare (eight-acre) hillside site, with fine views and woodland, Spring bulb and rose gardens, alongside herbaceous borders and ornamental ponds.

The garden is open every day, between 11am and 6pm from towards the end of March to the end of October and between 11am and 5pm in September and October.

Clacton-on-Sea

The discovery of fossilised bones of cave lion and straight-tusked elephant on the foreshore suggests that what became Clacton-on-Sea was part of an even sunnier 'Sunshine Coast' millions of years ago.

The original village developed into a 19th century seaside resort at a time when sea-bathing and coastal health were in fashion.

Clacton Pier

The pier, built in 1871, provides pure fun – spread over a total of 2.5 hectares (six acres).

There is a flight simulator, a 'seaquarium', music, fairground rides, side shows, haunted house, safari train, high-flying thrills, trampolines, a pub, two restaurants, take-aways, free deck chairs and baby changing facilities.

Entrance to the pier, which is open daily, is free (Telephone for latest times).

Magic City

A major Clacton entertainment centre for all the family, including an amusement centre with bingo, pool, snooker, ten pin bowling and a themed, arena laser game.

For younger children, there is an indoor adventure playground with a bouncy castle, tumble tower, tunnel tube and spider's web.

Magic City is open between 10am and 6pm daily.

Clacton Area

Beth Chatto Gardens

Exhibits by Beth Chatto, one of the region's most celebrated gardeners, have won her ten consecutive gold medals at the Chelsea Flower Show – as well as a Victoria Medal of Honour for outstanding services to horticulture.

The beauty of the gravel, water and woodland gardens at White Barn House, Elmstead Market, just north of Brightlingsea is that visitors can see a wide variety of plants growing in their natural environment.

The gardens and nursery are open between 9am and 5pm Monday to Saturday from the beginning of March to the end of October and between 9am and 4pm Monday to Friday from the beginning of November to the end of February (Closed Sundays and Bank Holidays).

Refreshments are available.

Clacton-on-Sea

Brightlingsea

Brightlingsea is a Maritime England Heritage Town and the location for several national and international sailing championships.

Fishing smacks and sailing barges are still here in their own dock and there is an annual Smack and Barge Race, which attracts entries from around the coast.

The town's **museum** depicts the industries, the people and events that have influenced the development of its domestic and working life – with education, the wars, town events, ties with the sea and leisure all covered.

It is open between 2pm and 5pm Monday to Thursday and 10am and 4pm on Saturdays from April to October (Other times by appointment).

Also worth a visit in Brightlingsea is the 13th century Jacobe's Hall – one of the oldest timber-framed buildings in England.

East Essex Aviation Society and Museum

The museum is located in the Martello Tower at Clear Point, near St Osyth.

It contains displays of wartime

Moulsham Mill
Tel. 01245 608200

RHS Garden Hyde Hall
Tel. 01245 400256

Clacton Pier
Tel. 01255 421115
Fax. 01255 222163
e-mail: e-harrison@
aspects.net

Magic City
Tel. 01255 421144

Beth Chatto Gardens
Tel. 01206 822007
Fax. 01206 825933

Brightlingsea Museum
Tel. 01206 303185 or
303384 (Curator)

**East Essex Aviation
Society and Museum**
Tel. 01255 428028

aviation, including artefacts from World War II crash sites, military and naval photographs, uniforms and other memorabilia.

The museum is open between 10am and 2pm on Sundays and 7 and 10pm on Mondays all year as well as on Wednesdays between 10am and 2pm from June to September and on all Bank Holidays.

Frinton-on-Sea

Frinton, with its tree-lined avenues sweeping down to the elegant esplanade and the greensward cliff path looking down on a splendid beach, is a haven of peace and quiet.

Walton-on-the-Naze

The word 'Naze' ('nez' in French or 'ness', as in Skegness) means 'nose' or 'headland'.

Today Walton is a model of an early Victorian seaside resort - its 1870 **pier** is the second longest in Britain – and is the stepping off place for the Backwaters, a national nature reserve.

Walton Pier
Tel. 01255 672288

St Osyth Social History Museum
Tel. 01255 820524 or 821012

Adventure Island
Tel. 01702 468023
Fax. 01702 601044

Southend Cliffs Pavilion
Tel. 01702 351135

Kursaal
Tel. 01702 322322
Fax. 01702 322387

Central Museum (and Planetarium)
Tel. 01702 215640

Beecroft Art Gallery
Tel. 01702 347418

Pier Museum
Tel. 01702 611214

Southchurch Museum
Tel. 01702 467671

St Osyth Priory

The village takes its name from St. Osytha, daughter of the Christian King of East Anglia, and the present Priory is built on the site of a nunnery founded by the Princess.

The village centre is dominated by the priory and the 12th century parish church. There is also a boatyard and water-skiing on the lake.

The village's **Social History Museum** houses artefacts, documents, photographs and sound recordings related to local social history.

Special exhibitions and opening times are advertised and other admission is by appointment only.

Southend-on-Sea

Southend is the largest town in Essex, has the longest pleasure pier in the world and was home to the world's first theme park.

It hosts the Southend Airshow (May), the London to Southend Classic Car Run (July), Carnival Week (August), Thames Sailing Barge Match (August) and the Southend Water Festival (September).

There is also championship Offshore Power Boat Racing, a Cricket Festival (August/ September), the Southend Classic 10K Road Race (October), Leigh Folk Festival (June) and Old Leigh Regatta (September).

Adventure Island

This island of fun has more than 40 rides and attractions for all ages.

It is open daily between 11am and late from Easter to mid-September and 11am and 6 or 8pm at weekends from October to March plus daily at Autumn Half Term and over Christmas Holidays.

Cliffs Pavilion

There is daily entertainment throughout the Summer season at the largest purpose-built performance arts venue in Essex.

Its 1630-seater auditorium hosts a year-round programme of top entertainment, including touring performances of West End musicals.

Kursaal

Kursaal, the world's first-ever theme park, was opened in 1901.

Originally intended as an entertainment venue with gardens, the 10 hectare (26-acre) site rapidly included the latest attractions and rides.

Before World War II, it was the fairground of London's East End and, during the war, it became a NAAFI stores for the South East.

The Kursaal has been reborn as a new millennium world of entertainment with attractions including tenpin bowling, a children's party centre, amusements, cafes, bars and restaurants.

It is open from 10am to late all year round.

Museums and Galleries

The Central Museum in Southend covers the human and natural history of the area and has the only Planetarium in the South East outside London.

Four centuries of art are on show in the **Beecroft Art Gallery,** while the **Pier Museum** tells the story of the world's longest pier and **Southchurch Hall Museum**

Kursaal, Southend-on-Sea

Old Leigh

displays period room settings – from the Middle Ages to Victorian times.

Prittlewell Priory Museum has an eclectic collection, ranging from early radios and televisions to wildlife and the history of the 12th century priory.

Contact the local tourist information centre for museum opening times.

Sea Life Aquarium

The Sea Life Aquarium gives visitors a divers-eye view of what goes on in an unfamiliar world beneath the waves.

Sea Life is open daily from 10am in Summer and between 11am and 3pm in Winter (weekends from 10am).

Southend Pier

The longest pleasure pier in the world – it stretches 2.14 kilometres (1.33 miles) into the Thames Estuary – was opened in 1889 and has survived both catastrophic fires and being hit by ships.

The nearby museum reveals the full story of the most famous pier on the planet.

Southend Pier is open between 8am and 9pm Monday to Friday and 8am and 10pm Saturday and Sunday from Easter to the beginning of October.

From October to Easter the times are 8am to 4pm Monday to Friday, and 8am to 6pm Saturday and Sunday.

Dutch Cottage

The Dutch Cottage at Rayleigh (Open Wednesdays between 1.30pm and 4.30pm by appointment) is an eight-sided building based on a design by 17th century Dutch settlers.

Hadleigh Castle Country Park

Hadleigh Castle, built for Edward III and immortalised by John Constable, overlooks the Essex Marshes and the Thames estuary.

The Country Park is made up of the castle ruins (open at any reasonable hour), fields and woodland and there is a guided tour programme throughout the year.

Norsey Wood Local Nature Reserve

In this peaceful area of traditional, coppiced woodland, Wat Tyler, leader of the Peasants' Revolt, and 500 of his men were massacred by King Richard's soldiers in 1381.

Guided tours of Norsey Wood are available in Spring and Summer.

Old Leigh

Old Leigh was a fishing and boat-building centre in the past.

Today, with its narrow, cobbled High Street and picturesque rows of weather-boarded fishermen's cottages on the cliffs, it has been lovingly restored.

The many attractions include **Leigh Heritage Centre** (opening times vary), the **Lynn Tait Gallery** (10am to 8pm Summer; 5pm Winter) and **Old Leigh Studios.**

Southend Pier

The Old House, Rochford

History is revealed in the lovingly restored rooms of this supposedly-haunted early 13th century house, which is now the district council offices.

The building is open between 2pm and 4.30pm every Wednesday by guided tour only.

Wat Tyler Country Park

The emphasis is on conservation and natural history in this 49 hectare (120-acre) area of parkland, bounded by water.

Yet, it is also home to the **National Motorboat Museum** (Open between 10am and 4pm Thursday to Monday and daily during school holidays), a marina and miniature railway.

Prittlewell Priory Museum
Tel. 01702 342878

Sea Life Aquarium
Tel. 01702 462400

Southend Pier
Tel. 01702 215620

Dutch Cottage (Rayleigh)
Tel. 01702 318150

Hadleigh Castle Country Park
Tel. 01702 551072

Hadleigh Castle
Tel. 01760 755161

Norsey Wood Local Nature Reserve
Tel. 01277 624553

Leigh Heritage Centre
Tel. 01702 470834

Lynn Tait Gallery
Tel. 01702 471737

Old Leigh Studios
Tel. 01702 470490

The Old House
Tel. 01702 318144

Wat Tyler Country Park
Tel. 01268 550088

National Motorboat Museum
Tel. 01268 550077

North Norfolk

An area of outstanding natural beauty, featuring a coastline which combines salt marshes with broad expanses of sandy beach and huge skies.

Inland from the scenic coast and towns like Cromer and Sheringham, there are charming small villages with traditional brick and flint buildings and welcoming hostelries.

Places for all the family to visit abound but the area appeals especially to artists, birdwatchers, naturalists and walkers, who visit in considerable numbers throughout the year.

There's always room to escape fellow human beings, however – if you choose.

Cley Mill and marshes

Tourist Information Centres

Aylsham
Tel. 01263 733903; Fax. 01263 733814

Cromer
Tel. 01263 512497; Fax. 01263 513613

Holt
Tel. 01263 713100

Mundesley (Seasonal)
Tel. 01263 721070; Fax. 01263 722796

Sheringham (Seasonal)
Tel. 01263 824329; Fax. 01263 821668

Ordnance Survey Maps
OS Landranger sheet numbers: 132, 133

Aylsham

A pleasant country town with an attractive market square and a good selection of shops and hostelries.

Black Sheep

An interesting retail outlet to be found in Penfold Street, Aylsham, just off the market place.

The shop – which is open between 9am and 5.30pm from Monday to Friday and 10am to 5pm on Saturday – features a wide range of products knitted from the fleeces of a flock of Black Welsh Mountain sheep kept nearby.

Bure Valley Railway

The Bure Valley, built in 1990, is Norfolk's longest narrow gauge heritage railway and one of the best of its kind in Britain.

Each year the 14.5 kilometre (nine mile), 38-centimetre (15-inch) gauge line attracts some 100,000 passengers, who travel through varied and attractive scenery between Aylsham and Wroxham on both steam and diesel trains.

The railway, which has intermediate stops at Brampton, Buxton and Coltishall, offers steam locomotive driving courses and also features a number of special events throughout the year.

The Aylsham station headquarters, a new building in the style of the Midland & Great Northern railway at the end of the Eighties, contains a tourist information centre and souvenir shop as well as the ticket office.

Aylsham Area

Alby Crafts

Craft centre located between Aylsham and Cromer and featuring the work of an assortment of artists and craftsmen and women as well as bottle and lace museums, tea rooms and gardens.

The centre is open daily (except

Blickling Hall

Mondays) from mid-March to Christmas and at weekends only for the rest of the year.

Blickling Hall

Blickling Hall – which was handed to the nation in 1940 – is one of England's great Jacobean houses and the supposed birthplace of Anne Boleyn.

Famed for its spectacular long gallery, superb library and fine collections of furniture, pictures and tapestries, it was regional winner of the NPI National Heritage Award for 1999/2000.

Blicking has richly-planted gardens, sweeping parkland and a traditional working estate of almost 2023 hectares (5000 acres).

The gardens are the vision of five different figures from the past, each modifying what had gone before. But it is the 1930s work of the influential garden designer Norah Lindsay that the National Trust has restored.

The Blickling estate extends to 1933 hectares (4777 acres) of which 1416 (3500) are farmland, 202 (500) woodland and 182 (450) parkland.

Public access is free and there are three way-marked walks, leaflets about which can be picked up from the estate barn.

The lake – formed before 1729, when it was called the 'New Pond' – was doubled in length in 1762 and is stocked with perch, pike, rudd and tench.

A number of activities and events – ranging from a balloon festival to bike rides and bird-watching, concerts, parades, performances of

Black Sheep Shop
Tel. 01263 733142 or 732006
Fax. 01263 734075

Bure Valley Railway
Tel. 01263 733858
Fax. 01263 733814
e-mail: info@bvrw.co.uk
web: www.bvrw.co.uk

Alby Crafts
Tel. 01263 761590

Blickling Hall
box office
Tel. 01263 738049
inquiries
Tel. 01263 738030
Fax. 01263 731660
e-mail:
abgusr@smtp.ntrust.org.uk
web:
www.nationaltrust.org.uk

Blickling Hall (Bailiff – for coarse fishing permits)
Tel. 01263 734181

Shakespeare plays and walks – are arranged at Blickling throughout the year.

The house at Blickling Hall is open daily – bar Mondays other than Bank Holidays and Tuesdays except in August – between 1pm and 5pm (last admission 4.30pm) from early April to the end of October.

The gardens are open during this same period between 10.30am and 5.30pm and between 11am and 4pm from November to March.

Morston harbour

Mannington Hall & Wolterton Park

Mannington Gardens and Countryside, eight kilometres (five miles) north-west of Aylsham, consists of a moated medieval manor house surrounded by beautiful gardens and grounds which include outstanding rose gardens and a lake.

The house is the private home of the Walpole family and is open only by appointment or for occasional charity events.

Wolterton boasts an 18th century mansion built in the 1720s for the younger brother of England's first Prime Minister, Sir Robert Walpole.

It is set in historic parkland, which includes a picnic area, and is open daily from 9am–5pm (or dusk, if earlier).

Wolterton organises a programme of special events and operates hall tours on Fridays between 2pm and 5pm (last tour 4pm) from April 28th.

There are more than 32 kilometres (20 miles) of waymarked footpaths around the Mannington and Wolterton Estate, which is open daily from 9am with the gardens open on Wednesdays, Thursdays and Fridays from June to August (11am–5pm) as well as Sundays (12 noon–5pm) from May to September.

Blakeney

Blakeney, was an important fishing and trading centre in the 13th and 14th centuries and there is evidence of boatbuilding in the village.

The so-called Point is owned by the National Trust and consists of a 5.5-kilometre (3½-mile) spit of sand and shingle with habitats ranging from dunes to salt marshes and mudflats.

This **National Nature Reserve** came into the Trust's ownership in 1912 as the first nature reserve in Norfolk, with the Point and surrounding marshes at Morston and Cley forming a protected conservation area of over 971 hectares (2400 acres).

Birds found there include a large colony of Sandwich Terns plus Common, Arctic and Little Terns, Oyster catchers and Ringed Plovers.

If you fancy a trip to see a colony of some 400 common and, usually darker, grey seals as well as bird life at the Point, the popular motor **boat trips** run by brothers John and Graham Bean and other operators could provide the answer.

Following in their father's footsteps, the Beans run boats for up to 40 passengers from Morston Quay, near Blakeney – where there is an information centre (as access to some areas of the Point is restricted during the nesting season).

Journeys are dependent on favourable tidal conditions but usually last between one and two hours, with a stop-over at Blakeney Point when tides are right.

Varying tide times and heights mean that each boat can make between two and four return journeys each day, at any time from 9.30am to 6pm.

The season is from April to the end of October although Winter trips are available by arrangement – the North Norfolk Coast can be a popular destination on a Winter's day.

Booking is advisable and sometimes essential.

Mannington Hall

Blakeney Area

Cley next the Sea

In the 15th and 16th centuries, Cley overlooked the vast Glaven river estuary and the marshes were covered at high tide – allowing boats access to a harbour near the church and beyond to Glandford.

In 1406 a vessel bearing James, son of Robert the Bruce, King of Scotland, was driven inshore by bad weather while on a voyage to France and he was detained by local seamen who sent him to London as a prisoner.

At one time Cley was the main port for Holt. But the river silted up to form an area of outstanding natural beauty.

Apart from a **smokehouse,** bakery and delicatessen, Cley also features a pottery producing a wide range of items and an art gallery and bookshop exhibiting work by well-known local artists.

The local Anglican church, St Margaret's, one of the Glaven Churches, was supposedly built in the reign of Henry VI and boasts a 13th century font.

Cley's early 18th century **Mill** is a well-known North Norfolk landmark and offers spectacular views across the salt marshes to the sea.

Last worked in 1920, it is now open to the public from Easter to the end of September and includes a small guest house with self-catering accommodation.

Cley Marshes, the oldest nature reserve in the country, has an international reputation as one of the best bird-watching sites in Britain.

It is owned by the Norfolk Wildlife Trust – formed as the Norfolk Naturalists' Trust in 1926 at the village's George and Dragon Hotel, which retains a close association and displays (on a brass church lectern) a 'Bird Bible' recording the sighting of rare species.

The Marshes, 0.8 kilometres (half a mile) east of Cley itself, are open all the year round except on Mondays (apart from Bank Holidays) and the visitor centre is open between 10am and 5pm from April to October.

Tickets must be obtained from the visitor centre or, out of season, from the warden at Watcher's Cottage, 200 metres from the car park in the direction of the village.

NB. The visitor centre and car park are both on the inland side of the A149 coast road.

Glandford

Natural Surroundings is a four hectare (ten-acre) wildlife garden and conservation centre opened near the village, four kilometres (three miles) from Holt, in 1989.

The River Glaven runs through the site, half of which is left in a natural state with an ancient water meadow traditionally maintained.

There is also a pond where youngsters can study the wildlife it contains and, in Spring, 'Bluebell Walks' are among the special activities run by the centre.

Natural Surroundings, which offers family passes and can arrange school visits, is open from Thursday to Sunday.

The village of Glandford itself is home to a tiny church which contains the delightful **Shell Museum** (open March to October from Tuesday to Saturday between 10am and 12.30pm/2pm and 4.30pm), containing the lifetime's collection of Sir Alfred Jodrell as well as other local artefacts.

Langham

Teams of craftsmen can be seen working with molten glass in this pretty village four kilometres (three miles) outside Holt.

Langham Glass, based in a restored 18th century barn complex, is one of the few traditional UK manufacturers left in this field and is unique in that everything is handmade and, therefore, each piece is different.

The company celebrated a famous victory in the Giftware Association's 'Gift of the Year 2000' competition after being placed on a short list of three from a vast list of entries.

The other finalists were Royal

Langham Glass

Cley Smokehouse
Tel. 01263 740282

Cley Mill
(Guesthouse)
Tel. 01263 740209

Cley Marshes Nature
Reserve (NWT)
Tel. 01263 740008

Natural Surroundings Centre
for Wildlife Gardening and
Conservation
Tel. 01263 711091

Shell Museum
Tel. 01263 740081

Langham Glass
Tel. 01328 830511
Fax. 01328 830787
e-mail:
LANGLASSOI@aol.com
web:
www.langhamglass.co.uk

Cley marshes

Worcester and a large company quoted on the New York stock market.

As well as commentaries from master glassmakers as they work, there are daily demonstrations of stained glass work (for which commissions are welcomed) and a museum and video also cover every aspect of the glass-making process.

There is a factory shop and also an antiques and collectable shop – selling everything from Dresden china to Lalique glass and an old beamed licensed restaurant.

Langham Glass is at The Long Barn, North Street, Langham, Norfolk, and is open to the public seven days a week all year round.

☎ ── FAX ── 💻

Cromer Pier Pavilion Theatre
bookings and information
Tel. 01263 512495
box office
Tel. 01263 512495
theatre
Tel. 01263 512281
Fax. 01263 515113

Cromer Museum
Tel. 01263 513543
Fax. 01263 511651
e-mail: alistair.murphy.
mus@norfolk.gov.uk
web: www.norfolk.gov.uk/
tourism/museums

Cromer

The annual 'Seaside Special', staged at Cromer's famous end-of-pier **Pavilion Theatre,** broke attendance records in 1999 – with 45,000 people enjoying 112 performances.

The show relies for its appeal on the versatility, enthusiasm and professionalism of an ensemble of lesser-known entertainers.

It runs from June to September, with a first programme continuing until the end of June and a second then taking over until the end of the season.

The Pavilion Theatre's Summer programme also includes a range of celebrity concerts, shows and events, taking in everything from ballet to comedy and a wide range of music from folk to opera, rock and swing.

Cromer also has a multi-screen cinema and – at the other end of the historic scale – a small **museum,** which is housed in a row of former fishermen's cottages and brings the people, natural history and geology of the area to life.

Visitors can see – illuminated by gaslight – the furnished 1890s home of a local fishing couple and find out about Henry Blogg's famous Cromer lifeboat rescues.

They can also take a look at crab fishing, and genteel holidays in Victorian 'Poppyland' – with bathing machines, costumes from neck to knee by law and mixed bathing frowned upon!

Or discover how the remains of the West Runton Mammoth, Britain's oldest and most complete elephant fossil, were recovered from the crumbling Norfolk cliffs.

A new, computerised, information base offers access to many of the museum's huge collection of historic photographs and illustrations of local people and places.

And the Beachcomber's Room – a discovery centre for children, complete with microscopes and other equipment, samples and suggested activities – can be booked for schools use.

There are a number of demonstrations and special walks with an historical or natural history emphasis during the year and regular family activity days during school holidays.

The museum is at East Cottages, Tucker Street – opposite the East end of Cromer Parish Church.

It is open all year between 10am and 5pm from Monday to Saturday and 2pm and 5pm on Sundays (Closed Monday 1–2pm, Christmas Day, Boxing Day and New Year's Day).

Facilities include a souvenir shop and toilets, although there is no disabled toilet facility and only the ground floor is accessible for wheelchair users.

There are large public car parks nearby. Follow signs on entering town.

Cromer sea front and pier

Felbrigg Hall

Cromer Area

Nearby Felbrigg Hall, owned by the National Trust, contains original 18th century furniture and features an outstanding library.

It is one of the finest 17th century houses in East Anglia and stands in its own 708 hectare (1750 acre) estate.

A dovecote and small orchard are to be found in the restored walled garden and the surrounding park is known for its woodland and lakeside walks which are open daily except for Christmas Day.

The house itself is open daily (except Thursdays and Fridays) between 1pm and 5pm (gardens 11am to 5.30pm) from the beginning of April to the end of October.

On Bank Holiday Sundays and Mondays the opening times for the house are between 11am and 5pm.

Holt

An historic Georgian town which acquired its name from the Saxon word for 'wood' and was recorded in the Domesday book as having a market and five watermills as well as – in Cley – its own port.

Since then, of course, the river has silted up. So Holt has no immediate port – nor does it have an open market any more.

But it still boasts considerable charm, a nationally-known public school in Gresham's and a nearby 40-hectare (100-acre) country park with facilities including signposted walks, a pond, children's play area and information centre.

The Holt Flyer is a family-run, independent bus service, which runs in conjunction with the North Norfolk Railway timetable and provides a connection between Holt station and the town centre, about 1.6 kilometres (one mile) away.

Its horsepower comes not from the internal combustion engine but from several trusty steeds – which share the role of pulling the three vehicles from the station to The Railway Tavern.

For details of the Flyer's journeys and costs contact Garry Thompson.

Also in Holt is the traditional, family-run, county department store of **Baker's and Larner's** – which has been trading in the High Street for almost four centuries.

Larners features an impressive food hall and also sells a wide range of other high quality products.

Holt Area

Kelling

Kelling Heath, near Holt, is home to the only **holiday park** in the country to employ a full time countryside manager.

Set in 101 hectares (250 acres) of woodland and heather, the park is a commercial venture with a campsite as well as permanently-sited caravan holiday homes and has been interna-tionally recognised for its contribution to Eco friendly tourism.

In 1999 it was named UK winner of the British Airways Tourism for Tomorrow Award and took the David Bellamy Gold Conservation award.

Kelling Heath, which is also holder of a silver award in the tourism industry's 'Oscars' – the England for Excellence honours – has an interesting diversity of flora and fauna as well as semi-ancient woodland and heathland.

The heather and grasses of the heathland are important because they provide a habitat for many different kinds of wildlife – such as common lizards, adders, spiders, wasps and stone chats.

Felbrigg Hall, Garden and Park
Tel. 01263 837444
Fax. 01263 837032
e-mail:
afgusr@smtp.ntrust.org.uk

Holt Flyer
Tel. 01263 712283

Baker's and Larner's of Holt
Tel. 01263 712244 or 712323
Fax. 01263 712720
e-mail: ctbaker@cwcom.net
web:
www.bakersofholt.co.uk

Kelling Heath Holiday Park
Tel. 01263 588181
Fax. 01263 588599

Conservation pond, Kelling Heath

Letheringsett Watermill

This Grade II listed mill in Riverside Road, is nearly 200 years old and is powered entirely by water from the adjacent River Glaven.

It is the only remaining working mill of its type in Norfolk with an 1827 iron water wheel casting and, for organic milling, blue quartz granite grind stones dating back to the Napoleonic wars.

The four storey mill features a small ground floor shop – where the flour and local hand-made breads and confectionery are available for sale – and, on the second floor, a picture and restoration room.

It is open to the public all year round between at least 10am and 5pm from Monday to Friday and 9am and 1pm on Saturdays and between 2pm and 5pm on Bank Holiday Sundays and Mondays.

Working demonstrations are also given daily (when open) between 2pm and 4.30pm in Summer and from Tuesday to Friday between 1.30pm and 3.30pm in Winter.

Visitors are welcome to stay at the mill or enjoy the river, millpond and ducks all morning or afternoon.

Muckleburgh

The Muckleburgh Collection is Britain's largest working military collection and was set up by Berrie Savory in the old NAAFI block of the

The Muckleburgh Collection

former army camp nestling at the foot of Muckleburgh Hill.

The site has a long history of military use going back as far as 1588, when it was fortified against the threat of the Spanish Armada.

Opened to the public by the Duke of Argyll in 1988, the collection has grown to include 16 working tanks, 120 military vehicles, guns and missiles and 2500 other exhibits.

The winner of numerous tourism awards, Muckleburgh has a licensed restaurant as well as a new and enlarged shop and offers full facilities for people with disabilities.

The Muckleburgh Collection at Weybourne Military Camp, Weybourne, Holt, Norfolk NR25 7EG – on the A149 coast road at Weybourne, about three kilometres (two miles) west of Sheringham and eight kilometres (five miles) north east of Holt – is open daily from 10am to 5pm between February and October.

Sheringham

The North Norfolk Railway is based at Sheringham station, close to the centre of this pretty seaside town.

Its headquarters are a short walk from the main line station on the regular Norwich – Sheringham

route, which has been described as one of the most picturesque lines in the country.

Attractions on site include a museum, signal box, display of locomotives and carriages, souvenir and model railway shop and buffet.

The Poppy Line, as it is known, is a friendly, full-size steam and diesel railway running though beautiful countryside by the sea.

It stretches for 8.5 kilometres (five and a quarter miles), between the seaside town of Sheringham and the small Georgian town of Holt, stopping at Weybourne and Kelling Heath Holiday Park (by request).

The line is part of the old Midland and Great Northern Joint Railway, opened on June 16th, 1887, and was closed down 40 years ago – before being resurrected by enthusiastic, steam-loving members of the M&GNJR Society.

Trains run every day from April to the end of September, with a limited service operating during all other months except January.

Special events – such as Thomas the Tank Engine days, a beer festival, Open Day, Diesel Gala, Model Railway Exhibition, Railway Gala and 1940s weekend – are held throughout the year.

Early December sees the start of the popular Santa Specials and the Mince Pie Specials are between

☎ ─ FAX ✎ 💻

Letheringsett Watermill
Tel. 01263 713153

Muckleburgh Collection
Tel. 01263 588210
Fax. 01263 588425
e-mail: jenny@
muckleburgh,demon.co.uk

North Norfolk Railway
Tel. 01263 822045
web: www.nnrailway.co.uk
talking timetable
Tel. 01263 825449
Pullman booking
Tel. 01263 822972 or
822045
Fax. 01263 823794

Christmas and New Year.

Sheringham offers the **Splash** centre, at Weybourne Road, Sheringham and has its own **Little Theatre,** in Station Road, which hosts plays, films, comedy, music and children's shows.

There is also a **museum** in Station Road, which is open between 10am and 4pm from Tuesday to Saturday and 2–4pm on Sundays from mid-April to the end of October.

Exhibits include items featuring the town's history and also a special display on the Weybourne elephant.

Sheringham Area

The Norfolk Shire Horse Centre

The Norfolk Shire Horse Centre features not only heavy horses and wagon rides but also extensive collections of farming bygones and farm and other animals.

There is a daily show programme, including harnessing and working horse demonstrations and special events days are organised throughout the year.

The centre is open between 10am and 5pm daily from April to October (Saturdays excepted – although open on Bank Holiday Saturday and other Saturdays throughout July and August).

Sheringham Park

The adjacent West Runton Riding Stables are open between 10am and 4pm daily except for Christmas Day, Boxing Day, New Year's Day and Mondays from November to February.

Sheringham Park

Travellers on the North Norfolk Railway can stop off at Weybourne Station (Tel. 01263 589800) and walk a short distance to Sheringham Park (in Upper Sheringham), well known for its fabulous scenery and coastal views.

The Park Estate, which extends to nearly 405 hectares (1000 acres) and was landscaped in the early 19th Century by Humphrey Repton, was acquired by the National Trust in 1986.

Described as 'the greatest of all English landscape gardeners', Repton spent most of his early life in Norfolk, saying that Sheringham possessed more natural beauty than any place he had ever seen.

The park has four main walks, some extending along coastal routes, and is famous for its rhododendrons, which cover a third of the estate.

The first is thought to have been planted in 1839 and today the collection, which is best seen in late May or early June, is 'one of the marvels of Norfolk'.

From the Gazebo viewing point, which is up a steep climb, visitors can see most of the estate including some 161 hectares (400 acres) of woodland.

The temple – designed back in the early 19th Century by Repton but not actually built until 1975! – was the last building to be added to the estate.

This point provides the best views over Sheringham Hall, which is now privately rented.

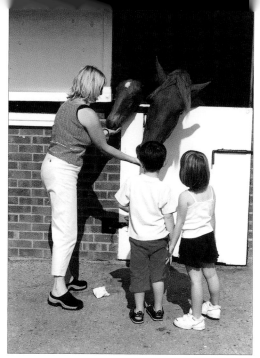

Norfolk Shire Horse Centre, West Runton

☎ FAX 🖥

Splash
Tel. 01263 825675
Fax. 01263 824288

Little Theatre
box office
Tel. 01263 822347
admin
Tel. 01263 822117
Fax. 01263 821963
e-mail: sherlit@
theatrel.freeserve.co.uk

Sheringham Museum
Tel. 01263 821871

Norfolk Shire Horse Centre & West Runton Riding Stables
Tel. 01263 837339
Fax. 01263 837132
web: www.norfolk-
shirehorse-centre.co.uk

Sheringham Park
seasonal information
Tel. 01263 821429
park warden
Tel. 01263 823778

The Park is open every day from dawn to dusk (dogs on leads admitted) and light refreshments are available from Easter to the end of September.

North-West Norfolk

North-West Norfolk is the land of national hero Admiral Nelson, Britain's first Prime Minister (Robert Walpole), agricultural reformer Thomas Coke and Queen Boudicca's Iceni tribe.

Its entire coastland is designated an Area of Outstanding Natural Beauty and within that belt are many important Sites of Special Scientific Interest.

The wildlife and bird reserves here are a major destination, or stopping off point, for hundreds of thousands of migrating birds – as well as bird watchers and beach-lovers who prefer solace to the crowds.

It is also a holiday destination for families who enjoy the more traditional seaside entertainment provided by resorts such as Hunstanton.

Tourist Information Centres

Hunstanton
Tel. 01485 532610; Fax. 01485 533972
e-mail: hunstanton.tic@west-norfolk.gov.uk

King's Lynn
Tel. 01553 763044; Fax. 01553 777281
e-mail: kings-lynn.tic@west-norfolk.gov.uk

Walsingham (Seasonal)
Tel. 01328 820510; Fax. 01328 820098

Wells (Seasonal)
Tel. 01328 710885; Fax. 01328 711405

Ordnance Survey Maps
OS Landranger sheet number: 132

The harbour, Brancaster Staithe

King's Lynn

Once known as 'the warehouse on the wash', Lynn is a major gateway into North-West Norfolk and has a maritime history stretching back more than 800 years.

Arts Centre

William Shakespeare is reputed to have acted here as a young man.

The Arts Centre is in the 15th century St George's Guildhall, the largest surviving medieval guildhall in England. It is also the heart of the famous King's Lynn Festival.

It is open between 10am and 2pm from Monday to Friday, except Good Friday, August Bank Holiday and Christmas and New Year holidays.

Caithness Crystal

Visitors can share in the secrets of the glassmaker at the Caithness Crystal Visitor Centre on King's Lynn's Hardwick Road.

They can take the free conducted tour and experience the heat and special atmosphere of the glasshouse as skilled craftsmen transform sand into exquisite glassware, using only the heat of the furnace and the skill of hand and eye.

The factory shop, licensed restaurant and glassmaking operations are open most days of the year.

Custom House

Local hero Admiral Nelson, smugglers, wealthy maritime merchants, fisherfolk – and Hollywood star Al Pacino – have all stood in the shadow of the Custom House.

The 17th century Henry Bell masterpiece overlooking the River Ouse is the town's best-known building.

Today visitors can wander through its famous Long Room, where 21st century displays tell of the town's seafaring history, its famous merchants, the customs' men and the rogues they chased – the smugglers of old Lynn.

There is a touch-screen, interactive computer display giving infor-

King's Lynn as a film set for the making of 'Revolution'

mation on some of Norfolk's famous seamen, including Lord Nelson and explorer Captain George Vancouver (born King's Lynn 1757), who gave his name to Canada's Pacific coastal city and island.

Built in 1683 and dominating Purfleet Quay, the Custom House was used when Al Pacino and an all-star cast were in Lynn on location for the Hollywood feature film Revolution.

The building is open from Easter to the end of October between 9.15am and 5pm from Monday to Saturday, 10am and 4pm on Sunday and daily between 10am and 4pm from November to Easter.

Green Quay

The recently restored 16th century Marriott's Warehouse on South Quay is home to this new environment attraction, which tells the story of the unique wildlife in the Wash through an exciting, interactive exhibition.

Visitors to Green Quay, which is open daily, can explore the aquaria and enjoy the films, while other facilities include a coffee house and shop.

King's Lynn Festival

The Festival was founded 50 years ago by the late Ruth, Lady Fermoy and the July Festival – a landmark

Arts Centre
(and King's Lynn Festival)
Tel. 01553 764864

Caithness Crystal
Tel. 01553 765111

Custom House
Tel. 01553 763044

Green Quay
Tel. 01553 662001

Old Gaol House
Tel. 01553 774297

event in the cultural life of Norfolk – is under the patronage of Queen Elizabeth, the Queen Mother.

It celebrated its 50th anniversary in 2000 with a typically wide range of the arts – from music in all its genres and literary events to art, film and poetry.

Old Gaol House

Adjoining the 15th century Trinity Guildhall, this is perhaps the town's spookiest tourist attraction.

Visitors will hear stories of the town's highwaymen, robbers and murderers of old and the sights, sounds and smells of prison life two centuries ago come to life with personal stereo tours.

The Gaol House is open daily between 10am and 5pm (last admission 4.15pm) from Easter to the end of October as well as on Mondays, Tuesday, Fridays and Sundays from November to Easter.

There is wheelchair access and a gift shop.

True's Yard

True's Yard is all that remains of King's Lynn's old fishing community.

It has been faithfully restored to tell the story of how people lived in those days and also offers research facilities for those wishing to trace their ancestry in King's Lynn, or for students researching the area.

True's Yard, which features a tea room and gift shop, is open daily, year round from 9.30am (Last entries 3.45pm). Ring for information on Christmas opening.

King's Lynn Area

African Violet Centre

The African Violet Centre at Terrington St. Clement has won ten Chelsea Flower Show Gold Medals, making the nursery and display house a tourist 'must' for all plant lovers.

The Centre is open between 10am and 5pm (or dusk if earlier) daily from early January to just before Christmas.

Castle Rising

An imposing 12th century Norman castle set in about five hectares (12 acres) of defensive earthworks.

African Violet Centre, Terrington St Clement

Castle Rising

This was where Isabella, the 'she-wolf' of France (Queen Isabella, Edward III's mother), was held prisoner after murdering her husband, Edward II. The views from the towering ramparts are spectacular.

The castle is open between 10am and 6pm daily from the beginning of April to the end of September, between 10am and 5pm daily throughout October and between 10am and 4pm on from Wednesday to Sunday only from the beginning of November to the end of March.

It is closed from December 24th to 26th and on January 1st.

Houghton Hall

Houghton – one of the grandest surviving Palladian houses in England – was built by Britain's first Prime Minister, Sir Robert Walpole, in the 1720s.

Walpole used the building to create a showcase for some of the period's finest architects, including James Gibbs and Colen Campbell.

The breathtaking interiors, especially the saloon, were the work of the illustrious William Kemp and the opulence of the furnishings reflects Walpole's importance.

Now lovingly restored to its former glory by the 7th Marquess of Cholmondeley, Houghton retains many of its original furnishings and visitors can enjoy it as it may have been in Walpole's day.

The 142-hectare (350-acre) property is home to more than 1000 white fallow deer.

Visitors can also inspect the model soldier collection (20,000 pieces), the walled garden – which has been recreated to feature an area devoted to fruit and vegetables – an herbaceous border, formal rose garden (more than 150 varieties), tea room and shop.

Houghton is open on Sundays, Thursdays and Bank Holiday Mondays from early in April until late September.

Sandringham House and Country Park

The Queen and Duke of Edinburgh's country retreat – set in 24 hectares (60 acres) of glorious informal gardens and 240 hectares (600 acres) of country park – is one of West Norfolk's crown jewels.

Sandringham House was built for King Edward VII and Queen Alexandra. The house is filled with mementoes, treasures and memories of four generations of the Royal Family.

The spectacular gardens include

rhododendrons, azaleas, camellias, magnolias, fuchsias and hydrangeas in season.

There are rare and historic trees, woodland and stream walks, King George VI's Garden and Queen Alexandra's Nest and Rockery Waterfall.

Garden tours are available at certain times of the year and private evening tours of the house can be arranged.

Facilities at the Visitor Centre, in the Country Park, include a restaurant and tea room, a gift shop, museum, Royal Gardens plant and flower stall, tractor and trailer tours, woodland and heath walks, scenic drives and picnic areas.

There is free car and coach parking.

Major annual events at Sandringham include the Country Weekend (July), Firework Concert (July), Flower Show (July) and Craft Fair (September).

The estate also runs the **Sandringham Shooting School,** catering for both novice and experienced shooters.

The house, museum and gardens are generally open between mid-April and late July, and between early August and early October (check for exact dates). The following opening times usually apply during these periods:

House – Daily between 11am and 4.45pm (closed Good Friday).

Museum – Daily between 11am and 5pm and also between 11am and 4pm at weekends in October (closed Good Friday).

Gardens – Daily between 10.30am and 5pm, also between 11 a.m and 4pm at weekends in October.

Visitor Centre – Daily from the beginning of April to the end of October (closed Good Friday), and then weekends only until Easter.

Hunstanton

This popular 19th century seaside resort – affectionately known as 'Sunny Hunny' – is the only holiday resort on the East Coast that actually faces west.

Boat Hire

A company called **W. J. Searle** offers guided boat tours, which leave from the town's Central Promenade.

Cruises are on a World War II amphibious D.U.K.W – the only commercially operated vehicle of its kind – or aboard the MFV Sea Lion.

Le Strange Old Barns, Old Hunstanton

Just 182 metres (200 yards) from Old Hunstanton Beach, this centre is believed to be the largest combined antiques, arts and crafts complex in Norfolk.

The centre is open daily between 10am and 5pm in British Winter Time (closed Christmas Day) and between 10am and 6pm in British Summer Time.

Oasis

Hunstanton's all-weather, sea front leisure centre is based on a tropically-heated leisure pool with aqua slide, giant inflatables, Jacuzzi and a range of swimming sessions and 'dry' activities.

Pool use is reserved for particular groups at certain times of the day (Please ring the Oasis for details and opening times).

Sea Life Aquarium

Sharks, starfish, octopus, eels and seals... this attraction takes visitors into a breathtaking but unfamiliar world beneath the waves, without anyone putting a toe in the water.

The attraction has a full programme of feeding demonstrations, talks and special presentations.

The Sea Life Aquarium also includes a special hospital with a sick bay for seals, some of which

Sea Life Aquarium, Hunstanton

True's Yard
Tel. 01553 770479

African Violet Centre
Tel. 01553 828374

Castle Rising
Tel. 01553 631330

Houghton Hall
Tel. 01485 528569

Sandringham
Tel. 01553 772675

Sandringham Shooting School
Tel. 01485 540255
Mobile 0831 673465

Searle's Boat Hire
Tel. 01485 535455
Mobile 0831 321799

Le Strange Old Barns
Tel. 01485 533402

Oasis
Tel. 01485 534227

Sea Life
Tel. 01485 533576
Fax. 01485 533531
web: www.sealife.co.uk

draw such a response from visitors that they decide to 'adopt' the animals.

Opening times at the Sea Life aquarium are normally between 10am and 6pm (later during Summer) every day except Christmas Day – but please check Winter opening times before visiting.

Brancaster Staithe

Bircham Mill

Visitors can climb to the top of this working mill – which was built in 1846 – and, on windy days, the sails will turn the milling machinery inside.

In the bakery is a 200-year-old oven that was capable of baking a hundred loaves at once. It is 2.5 metres (8 feet) wide and nearly 4 metres (12 feet) deep.

The tearoom (recommended by Egon Ronay) serves a selection of home-made cakes, cream teas, sandwiches and coffee.

The mill is open between 10am and 5pm daily during school holidays – and every Wednesday, Thursday, Friday, Saturday and Sunday from mid-April to the end of September.

Brancaster

The Royal West Norfolk Golf Club, a right royal challenge for anyone who loves links courses, surrendered its first hole to the sea in 1939 and has lost others since.

The club – and the popular beach alongside - are reached by a twisting road (subject to regular flooding at high tide) across the marshes.

At the eastern end of Brancaster is the site of a Roman 'Saxon shore' fort, Branodunum. Nothing is visible at ground level but aerial photography has revealed its shape in detail and there is an explanatory legend on site.

Brancaster Staithe

From the harbour at West Norfolk's sailing capital, there are views across the saltmarsh to Scolt Head.

A Site of Special Scientific Interest, Scolt is known especially for its nesting colonies of sandwich and common and little terns and is also a first landing spot for many rare migratory birds.

There are **ferries** to the island from both Brancaster Staithe and Burnham Overy Staithe.

Holme Dunes Nature Reserve

This nature reserve, close to the Norfolk Coastal Path between Holme and Thornham, is a Norfolk Wildlife Trust property.

Comprising saltmarsh, dune, scrub and pinewood, it includes trails, a visitor centre, hides, a beach sanctuary and a Norfolk Ornithological Association reserve.

Holme 'Seahenge'

In the Spring of the year 2050 BC, a great oak tree was cut down and its upturned stump was then half-buried on a site that is now part of the beach at Holme-next-the-Sea.

The following year, a number of smaller oaks were felled, cut into 56 posts and arranged in a circle around the stump.

Over the years, time and tide buried the construction beneath the shifting sands…

Nearly 4000 years later, the site was uncovered by the sea again and the whole area was examined and recorded by archaeologists.

The timbers were dug up and taken away for examination at the Flag Fen Laboratories – a Bronze Age site near Peterborough (q.v.). It was there that the main oak was dated so accurately, using carbon and tree ring-dating techniques.

Archaeologists are still not sure what 'Seahenge' was. But suggestions so far include a ceremonial site of one kind or another, perhaps with some astronomical significance, or a place where the dead were laid to speed body decomposition – so letting the spirit quickly find its way to the afterlife.

Norfolk Lavender

The Roman word for lavender is 'lavandum' – which literally means 'fit for washing'.

Today soap is just one of the many uses for lavender, which is not a native plant and is thought to have been introduced by the Romans.

Caley Mill at Heacham is home to 'England's lavender farm' and the site of a National Collection of Lavenders.

Guided tours for coach parties and other visitors take place regularly from May to the end of September.

At lavender harvest-time, visitors can visit the distillery – which contains two stills made in 1874 – to see the ancient process of extracting lavender oil from the florets.

Norfolk Lavender – which has a gift shop, a nursery area and tearoom – is open all year (except January 1st and December 25th/ 26th). Entrance is free.

Snettisham

Snettisham is famous as the site where more than a hundred Iceni/

Norfolk Lavender, Heacham

IronAge torcs have been found – most of them in a single field.

The torcs are heavy rings of twisted gold or silver – or an alloy of both (electrum) – and were probably worn about the neck.

Snettisham Nature Reserve

The RSPB's Snettisham nature reserve stands beneath a vital section of the 'East Atlantic Flyway' – one of the natural world's great migration routes, stretching from Arctic Greenland and Siberia to the coastline of Africa.

Up to 300,000 birds are present around the Wash in Winter and nearly a third of them land at Snettisham.

The Snettisham reserve has four hides and extends to 1630 hectares (4028 acres) of inter-tidal habitats and gravel pits.

April and May are the busiest months of the Spring migration – with vast flocks of waders which have wintered here departing for their northern breeding grounds and wave after wave of Summer migrants arriving from the south.

When there is a high tide and the flats are completely covered, the birds fly over to the neighbouring man-made gravel pits and islands to feed. As soon as the tide recedes, they return to the mud flats.

One of many events organised by the RSPB is a gathering to witness the breathtaking spectacle of tens of thousands of wading birds retreating from the mudflats and flying inland to their high tide roost.

Visitors are reminded that mudflats and salt marshes can be very hazardous places and they should take advantage of local advice (Tides tables are available from the reserve).

Snettisham is open at all times, and admission is free. Disabled visitors may, by prior arrangement with the warden, drive to the first hide.

Snettisham Park Farm

The hugely popular 130-hectare (320-acre) farm is visited by more than 60,000 people each year.

In season, children can help farm staff bottle feed the lambs, kid goats and piglets and say hello to a host of friendly farm animals.

Animal feeding times are 8.30am for calves and 11.30am, 2pm and 4pm for lambs, which are born around the end of March.

Visitors can try their hand at 'throwing' a pot, explore the huge adventure playground or take a safari (February to October) and see the famous Park Farm red deer herd, featuring some 60 hinds and three stags.

Other attractions include horse and pony rides, an archaeologist's trail and a gift shop and tea room.

Park Farm is open daily between 10am and 5pm from the beginning of February to the end of October and on Fridays, Saturdays and Sundays only between 10am and 3pm from the beginning of November to the end of January (Closed Christmas Day and Bank Holidays around that period).

Thornham

One of the most painted scenes in North-West Norfolk is Thornham's Coal Barn, where cargoes of coal from ships which sailed into the harbour were stored in olden times.

The rusted up sluice, nearby, kept the channel to the sea clear – its gate dropped at high tide to trap great quantities of water in the lagoon behind.

At low tide, the sluice would be opened and the water rushed down to the sea, clearing the channel as it went.

The beach at Thornham – another famous village location is the Lifeboat Inn – is almost invariably a place of great solitude and natural beauty in both Winter and Summer.

Titchwell Marsh Nature Reserve

Bircham Mill
Tel. 01485 578393

Royal West Norfolk Golf Club
Tel. 01485 210223

Scolt Head Ferry
Tel. 01485 210456
(G.Witiker) or 01485 210638
(M. Nudds)

Holme Nature Reserve (NWT)
Tel. 01603 625540

Norfolk Lavender
Tel. 01485 570384
Fax 01485 571176
e-mail: admin@norfolk-lavender.co.uk

RSPB Snettisham Nature Reserve
Tel. 01485 542689

Park Farm
Tel. 01485 542425
web: www.norfolkbroads.com/parkfarm

Tichwell Marsh Nature Reserve (Visitor Centre)
Tel. 01485 210779

Titchwell Marsh Nature Reserve

The RSPB's Titchwell Marsh reserve covers a multitude of habitats.

In Spring, the Titchwell reedbeds are alive with song as migrant reed and sedge warblers arrive to join the

Burnham Overy

resident reed buntings.

About 20 pairs of bearded tit nest here too, bitterns are seen regularly and marsh harriers nest in the reeds.

In one of the lagoons – which are used mostly by migrating waders, nesting black-headed gulls, teal, gadwalls and other ducks – the reserve mixes seawater with freshwater to create a special habitat where up to 40 avocets nest.

Titchwell Marsh Nature Reserve is open daily all year around except for Christmas Day and Boxing Day.

The paths and hides are open all the time and there is wheelchair access.

Wells-next-the-Sea

A charming little harbour town at the heart of the Norfolk Heritage Coast, Wells is famed for its superb beaches, mysterious marshes, its birdlife, tourist shops and entertainment centres.

Maritime Museum

The old RNLI Lifeboat House, built in 1868 and now listed as of historic interest, is an apt home for the Wells Maritime Museum.

Displays include histories of Wells' lifeboats, famous floods, the harbour and smuggling and there are also exhibits about fishing, natural history and wildfowling.

Wells and Walsingham Light Railway

The town is home to the Wells & Walsingham Light Railway – the world's longest 10¼-inch gauge passenger-carrying steam railway –

Peddars Way and Norfolk Coast Path

Revenge was swift once the Romans recovered from Colchester, Roman London and St Albans being burned to the ground by the fiery-headed Queen Boudicca in the Iceni revolution of AD60.

The building of Peddars Way as a Roman Road was probably designed to keep the West Norfolk Iceni territories within fast chariot distance.

Today, the 74 kilometre (46-mile) Peddars Way and 75 kilometre (47-mile) Norfolk Coast Path join to form a 150 kilometre (93-mile) National Trail.

The Norfolk Coastal Path

The path starts in Hunstanton and takes a winding track via the wild and untamed coastline – and some short sections of road – to Holme, Thornham, Brancaster, Brancaster Staithe, Burnham Deepdale, Burnham Overy, Holkham, Wells, Blakeney, Cley-next-the-Sea, Sheringham and Cromer.

Peddars Way

The path begins amid conifer forests near Thetford on

Knettishall Heath on the Norfolk/Suffolk border.

Its trail then travels north, across the sand and flint of Breckland, skirting the edge of the Ministry of Defence Battle Area and passing near Grime's Graves, a Neolithic flint mining site. The track passes just east of Swaffham before continuing its lonely, often hauntingly beautiful, path via Castle Acre, Great Bircham, Sedgeford and Ringstead to the coast at Holme.

That's the junction where the Peddars Way meets the Hunstanton to Cromer Norfolk Coast Path.

The gentle terrain of the Peddars Way makes this walk particularly suitable for disabled people. There are several stretches to be enjoyed by those in wheelchairs, with frames or sticks (Details of locations on Countryside Commission map).

Walkers may feel that the track can be remote – particularly the latter stages of Peddars Way – with hardly a house in sight for much of the distance. But they are never that far from a minor diversion to link up with a bus service.

which has halts at Warham St Mary and Wighton and the pilgrimage village of Walsingham as its destination.

The service runs daily between Easter and the end of October.

Wells-next-the-Sea Area

Burnham Market

There are – depending on the way you count them – seven or eight Burnham parishes.

The biggest, Burnham Market, is a sophisticated tourist village with some fascinating shops, distinctive restaurants and a famous hostelry – **The Hoste Arms.**

Burnham Thorpe

England's greatest naval hero, Admiral Lord Horatio Nelson – whose father, Edmund, was Rector here between 1755 and 1802 – was born in the village in 1758.

The old Rectory where Nelson was

Wells and Walsingham Light Railway

born has long been torn down and replaced by another building. But there is a plaque on the wall by the road, marking the place where it stood.

The village's **Lord Nelson pub** is a major attraction for Nelson enthusiasts. It has no bar, as was traditional in olden times, and serves a distinctive tipple known as 'Nelson's Blood'.

The recipe is said to be a secret. But some who have drunk it – and survived – say the basic ingredients are 100% Navy rum and alcoholic cloves.

Nelson held a farewell party in the pub (then named The Plough) before taking command of one of his first big ships. It was renamed The Lord Nelson two years after the Admiral's death at the Battle of Trafalgar.

Holkham

If Admiral Nelson belongs to Burnham Thorpe, Coke of Norfolk (1754 – 1842) is linked forever with Holkham Hall – although he did not actually build the place.

Coke introduced new breeding techniques and he and fellow Norfolkman, 'Turnip' Townshend also brought in new root crops. Their part in the Agricultural Revolution helped put Norfolk at the cutting edge of agricultural reform.

It also enabled Coke to raise his total tenancy rents from £2200 to £22,000 a year between 1776 and 1816.

Coke of Norfolk, who became Earl of Leicester (second creation), was the great nephew and heir of Thomas Coke (1697–1759), later Earl of Leicester (first creation).

He it was who started work on Holkham Hall in 1734 although it was not finished until 1762 – after the Earl's death.

Today the 18th Palladian-style stately home, situated in a magnificent 1200 hectare (3000 acre) deer park, offers the visitor 300 years of history in a day.

Its attractions range from artworks by Rubens, Van Dyke and Gainsborough, the stunning grandeur of the Marble Hall, the magnifi-

Holkham Hall

cent State Rooms and fascinating old kitchen to the Bygones Museum, pottery shop, nursery, art gallery and stables restaurant.

Visitors can also stroll down to Holkham beach, where scenes for 'Shakespeare in Love' were filmed.

For opening times, contact Holkham Hall.

Walsingham

Once known as 'the holiest place in England', Walsingham boasts both **Anglican and Roman Catholic shrines.** It has been a famous place of Christian pilgrimage since 1061, when the lady of the manor had a vision in which the Blessed Virgin asked her to build, in Little Walsingham, a replica of Nazareth's Holy House.

Before long, word of the vision and the resulting building spread widely, with pilgrims travelling from all over the country to visit 'Little Nazareth'.

It was so famous that visitors included Henry II, Edward I and III and the prince who was later to become Henry VIII.

Individual visitors are received at the Shrines every day and **guided tours** of the area are available in the Summer.

At Little Walsingham there is a **Shirehall Museum** with Georgian Courthouse and **Abbey grounds** open between 10am and 4.30pm from Monday to Saturday during the Summer.

Wells Maritime Museum
Tel. 01328 711646

Wells & Walsingham Light Railway (Talking timetable)
Tel. 01328 710631

Hoste Arms
Tel. 01328 738257

Lord Nelson (Burnham Thorpe)
Tel. 01328 738241

Holkham Hall
Tel. 01328 710227
Fax. 01328 711707

Walsingham Anglican Shrine Office
Tel. 01328 820255 or 821073

Walsingham Roman Catholic Pilgrim Bureau
Tel. 01328 820217
Fax. 01328 821087

Walsingham Guided Tours
Tel. 01328 820250

Little Walsingham Shirehall Museum and Abbey Grounds
Tel. 01328 820510
Fax. 01328 820098
e-mail:
walsingham.museum@
farmline.com

Peddars Way and Norfolk Coast Path
Tel. 01328 711533
Fax. 01328 710182
e-mail: peddars.way@
dial.pipex.com

Mid-Norfolk

Small but busy market towns set in peaceful countryside typify this particular area of Norfolk.

For anyone with an interest in history, attractions include museums of gas, local history and rural life, preserved railways, Norman and Saxon ruins and famous shrines.

For those with more modern interests, there is a delightful collection of mechanical organs to be tracked down while fans of new technology can check out an award-winning environmental centre which features the largest wind turbine in the country.

Tourist Information Centres

Dereham
Tel. 01362 698992

Fakenham (Seasonal)
Tel. 01328 850102; Fax. 01328 850103

Swaffham
Tel. 01760 722255 (Seasonal – answerphone when closed); 722504 or 723636 (Out of season)

Ordnance Survey Maps
OS Landranger sheet numbers: 132, 143, 144

EcoTech, Swaffham

East Dereham

A bustling market town whose famous former residents include the author George Borrow and poet William Cowper.

Also remembered here is Saint Withburgha, a princess who was the youngest daughter of the King of the East Angles but gave up her regal life to be poor and made the town a place of pilgrimage.

A well named after her can be found immediately west of the parish church of St Nicholas – at what is said to have been her original burial place before her bones were moved to Ely.

Bishop Bonner's Cottage Museum

Housed in a timber-framed cottage in Saint Withburga's Lane, this small museum is named after a 16th century Rector of Dereham who went on to become Bishop of London.

It contains a collection of local exhibits including clothes from the Victorian era, domestic and farm implements and toys.

The museum is open from Tuesday to Friday between 2.30pm and 5pm and on Saturdays between 3pm and 5.30pm from May to October.

Dereham Windmill

Built in 1836, this corn mill on the edge of town was bought by Breckland District Council for a token £1 in 1979 – although, by then, much of the original machinery had been removed.

Inside, visitors can see what remains of the machinery and a display of photographs of other East Anglian mills, while outside there is a car park and landscaped picnic area.

East Dereham Area

Foxley Wood

Believed to be 6000 years old, Foxley is Norfolk's largest ancient woodland, with magnificent tall oaks.

Spring is an especially good time to visit, as the birds, butterflies and wildflowers – including blue tits, robins, thrushes and woodpeckers, brimstone and orange-tip butterflies and water avens or early purple orchid – are then at their most colourful.

But the wood – which is open from 10am to 5pm all year round – is a good place to unwind in any season.

Historic Railways

There are two privately-owned local railways – the **Mid Norfolk Railway** and the Yaxham Light Railway.

The MNR, owned by a preservation trust, is based at The Railway Station, Station Road, Dereham, Norfolk NR19 1DF.

It runs through almost 18 kilometres (11 miles) of typical rural Norfolk, linking many small villages and hamlets with the towns of Wymondham and Dereham.

A diesel railcar service operates three times daily in each direction on Saturdays, Sundays and Bank Holidays as well as on Wednesdays in July and August.

Plans are also afoot to re-open County School, a Victorian rural station just over nine kilometres (six miles) beyond Dereham and close to the village North Elmham.

There are parking facilities, toilets and a picnic site at County School, which is signed from the B1110 road, and a tearoom and shop operate during the Summer months.

A number of special events are held on the railway – which has disabled access to some trains and special toilet facilities at Dereham – throughout the year (Please phone for details).

At Dereham, refreshments and snacks are available, there is a shop which sells souvenirs, gifts and guide books and various items of rolling stock can be seen in the station yard.

The licensed Puffers Bar opens in a restored railway carriage on Fridays, Saturdays, Sundays and Bank Holidays.

The MNR Wymondham Abbey Station, a newly-built halt, is close to the historic and impressive Abbey,

Saint Withburgha's Well, East Dereham

Foxley Wood (NWT)
Tel. 01603 625540
Fax. 01603 630593

Mid Norfolk Railway
Tel. 01362 690633
Fax. 01362 698487
e-mail:
admin@mnrpt.freeserve.co.uk
web: www.mnr.org.uk/

while the award-winning mainline Wymondham Station is just 20 minutes walk away.

The latter – part of the national rail network – houses the well-known Brief Encounter tearooms and other railway-themed displays.

The Yaxham Light Railway, at Station Road, Yaxham, near Dereham, Norfolk NR19 1RD, is a 24-inch narrow gauge railway with both diesel and steam locos and rolling stock mainly from slate quarries.

Public access to this, however, is normally only possible through the MNR.

Details of other activities and attractions in the Dereham area can be obtained from Dereham Tourist Information Centre, which is open from Monday to Saturday between May and September at at The Bell Tower, Church Street, Dereham.

Norfolk Rural Life Museum

This former Poor House at Beech House, Gressenhall, is a working reminder of past days and ways in the countryside.

There are displays covering village life, cottages, rural trades and crafts, farming – Gressenhall's Union Farm is worked with horses and stocked with rare breeds of cattle (Red Polls), pigs (Large Blacks) and sheep (Norfolk Horn) – and working on the land.

Suffolk Punches are used for ploughing, cultivating, muck-spreading and pulling wagons full of corn at harvest time.

The horses, weighing in at around a ton with short, powerful legs and thick chests, are extremely rare nowadays. There are thought to be no more than 400 of them in the whole of Britain.

Between 1777, when the workhouse opened, and 1948 when it finally closed, as many as 670 people at a time lived there and life for the inmates was hard and monotonous with diet meagre and meals eaten in silence in the dining hall.

Discipline in the workhouse was strict – solitary confinement for periods up to 12 hours on a diet of bread and water was normal for minor offences.

The workhouse was run very much like a prison and conditions had to be sufficiently uninviting to deter all but the utterly destitute from seeking admission.

The surrounding outbuildings, now Craftsmen's Row, were also used

Norfolk Rural Life Museum, Gressenhall

to accommodate paupers – but only 'casuals', who stayed for a day or so.

Later, the outbuildings offered accommodation to those considered unsuitable to reside in the main building – such as unmarried mothers and lice carriers.

Today, there are several recreated workshops in each of the rooms – an old fashioned bakery, a village shop, a blacksmith's, a saddlery, a wheelwright's and a basket-weaving workshop.

Cherry Tree Cottage at Gressenhall is a replica of a typical Edwardian farm labourer's cottage of around 1910.

It was originally built in 1853 as a ward for respectable aged married couples and has four rooms including the kitchen, which contains a wrought iron range still used for cooking demonstrations for visiting school children.

Gressenhall organises day schools for adults as well as special activities for schools, families and general visitors – such as an adventure play area, cart rides, haymaking demonstrations, farm and workhouse talks, quizzes and quests.

It features farm, woodland and riverside trails and also has an ongoing conservation programme, which includes hedge and tree planting.

The Rural Life Museum, nearly five kilometres (three miles) north west of Dereham and three kilometres (two miles) from the A47 on the B1146, reopened to the public in April 2000 after extensive redevelopment paid for by more than £1½ million of National Lottery funding.

Facilities include a large souvenir shop, cafeteria, gardens, toilets, disabled toilets and wheelchair access.

There are car and coach parks on site and disabled badge holders may drive up to the front entrance by prior arrangement. Guide dogs only are admitted.

The museum is open from the beginning of April until the last Sunday in October between 10am and 5pm from Monday to Saturday and 12 noon to 5.30pm on Sundays.

North Elmham

Small village with the remains of a Saxon Cathedral and earthworks as well as a 13th century church.

Fakenham

A small market town which boasts evidence of Saxon settlement in the 6th century and John O'Gaunt as its 14th century Lord of the Manor.

Although its main industry throughout much of the 20th century was printing, the main employers today are a confectionery firm and the company which produces Linda McCartney's frozen vegetarian meals.

Fakenham Market

A regular Thursday event which brings a bustle to the town centre from early in the morning until mid-afternoon.

Fakenham Museum of Gas and Local History

The only surviving – and substantially complete – example in England and Wales of a small, hand-fired gas works.

Even at the peak of gas production, the 19th century gas holder and buildings served just 500 customers in the town and employed seven men.

Displays of domestic gas appliances – including old cookers, fires, irons, kettles and lamps – can be seen as well as the buildings and equipment and an old-fashioned gas lamp stands in the courtyard.

The museum – which is open on Thursdays only from the end of May to the beginning of September – also features a display of local items from the past, which give an interesting insight into the life and history of the town over the years.

Fakenham Racecourse

National Hunt meetings are held in the Spring and Winter at this course, which has been in existence since 1902.

Pensthorpe Waterfowl Trust

Fakenham Area

Dinosaur Adventure Park

Boasting one of the world's largest collections of life-size dinosaurs, this attraction can be found at Weston Park, Lenwade – between Norwich and Fakenham – off the main A1067 Fakenham road.

Apart from a dinosaur trail, it features a woodland maze, deer safari, crazy golf course, education centre, picnic and play areas, dinostore and diner, plus 'Climb-a-saurus' – a 23-metre (75-ft) activity dinosaur containing conventional and rope ladders, a scramble net and slides.

The park is open between at least 10am and 4pm on Fridays, Saturdays and Sundays from the end of March to the end of October as well as on the remaining days of the week from early May to early September.

Pensthorpe Waterfowl Trust

Founded by 68-year-old waterfowl enthusiast Bill Makin, who farmed at Pensthorpe for 50 years and started to convert old gravel sites in 1976, using the River Wensum to fill the disused pits.

Pensthorpe is home to 120 species of waterfowl, both European and non-European, including ducks, geese, goldeneye, ibis, pochard, shovellers, spoonbills and various waders.

In addition to the waterways, the reserve – which stretches over 186 hectares (460 acres) of prime Norfolk countryside and attracts some 40,000 visitors each year – includes woodland, meadowland, scrubland, aviaries, a raised dipping pool for children and an education centre.

There is a heated observation gallery offering an excellent view of waterfowl in the lakes and a woodland hide from which visitors can see wild birds like woodpeckers, blue tits, willow tits and nuthatches feeding.

One of the latest attractions at Pensthorpe is the New Millennium Garden – the latest (and largest!) project undertaken by Dutch landscape designer Piet Oudolf.

The idea for the garden, which consists of just under half a hectare (one acre) of natural planting and was officially opened in August 2000, arose around 1997, when Oudolf started the project on paper.

Planting began in May 1999 and when Oudolf himself arrived at the site he brought with him an entourage of 12,500 plants.

The result is a landscape billowing with colour, anchored by structure and graced by grasses down to the lakeside.

Award-winning facilities for the disabled at the park – which organises a number of special events in the Summer – include a designated parking area, accessible toilets and a network of hard-surfaced pathways offering easy access to the water's edge.

Pensthorpe Waterfowl Trust, on the A1067 south east of Fakenham, Norfolk, is open between at least 10am and 4.30pm, seven days a week for most of the year (week-ends only from January to mid-March).

The Thursford Collection

Located at Thursford Green, near Fakenham, Thursford features a unique collection of mechanical organs as well as a Gondola Switch-back roundabout ride and restored traction engines.

Daily live musical shows at Thursford – which is open between 12 noon and 5pm from Good Friday to October 22nd – feature the organ collection and The Wurlitzer Show.

The attraction also features ornaments, brass and crafts in a stable gift shop, a picture gallery, ice cream parlour and tea room.

Swaffham

Another attractive small market town with an unusual, triangular-shaped market place.

Swaffham pedlar John Chapman walked all the way to London Bridge after dreaming that he would find his fortune there.

Instead, he met a man there who

Rural Life Museum
Information line
Tel. 01362 860385
general museum inquiries
Tel. 01362 860563
educational facilities
Tel. 01362 860294
Fax. 01362 860383
web: www.norfolk.gov.uk/
tourism/museums/nrlm.htm

Gas Museum
Tel. 01328 855597

Race Course
Tel. 01328 862388
Fax. 01328 855908

Dinosaur Park
Tel. 01603 870245
web:
www.dinosaurpark.co.uk

Penstorpe
Tel. 01328 851465
Fax. 01328 855905
e-mail: enquires@
pensthorpe.sagehost.co.uk

Thursford
Tel. 01328 878477

The Thursford Collection

Castle Acre Priory

said he had also had a dream – a dream that if he dug under a pear tree in a Swaffham, he would find treasure.

Chapman returned to Swaffham and dug up his fortune. Today there is a carving of John Chapman, his wife and dog in Swaffham Church.

Swaffham's famous open-air Saturday morning market – usually up and running by 6.30am and fairly busy by 8am – and lively public auctions attract thousands to the town.

The stars and crew of the 'Allo 'Allo television series found it a pleasant place to stay too – following in the footsteps of the Dad's Army team who visited on location work.

In the market place stands the Market Cross, presented to the town by the Earl of Orford in 1783. On the top is a statue of Ceres, the Roman God of the harvest.

Perhaps Ceres understood that old Norfolk agricultural saying: "I went to Swarf'am, a traashin' fer naathen" – loosely translated as: "I went to Swaffham a threshing the corn for no pay."

Nelson – and indeed Lady Hamilton – are claimed to have been regular visitors to Montpelier House, one of the fine Georgian buildings around the market place, in the 18th century.

EcoTech

Anyone who thinks Nelson's Column in Trafalgar Square is tall, has obviously never seen the UK's largest single wind turbine – it is almost twice the height.

The wind turbine, which dominates Swaffham's EcoTech – the pioneering new environmental discovery centre – is capable of generating 1,500,000 watts of clean power. That's enough to meet half of Swaffham's needs.

Visitors can climb the 300 steps to the top for a panoramic view of the Norfolk landscape from the glass-walled viewing platform.

EcoTech, run by an educational charity which aims to stimulate and inform people about the need for sustainable development, is housed in an award-winning state-of-the-art timber-framed building – the largest in East Anglia.

It boasts computer-controlled heating and cooling systems using solar panels and a biomass boiler fuelled by locally-sourced wood chips as well as a rainwater recycling scheme.

Inside the centre, EcoTech features the 4 billion year-old story of Earth, from stardust to planet and – very recently in time terms – the arrival of plants, animals and the human race.

A complex interactive area gives youngsters a new look at some of the problems facing Earth today.

Also on site are a terraced café, organic gardens, wildlife areas and other displays.

It adds up to a 'must' day out that will leave both young and old with some possible solutions for a planet that could be in trouble.

EcoTech is open daily between 10am and 5pm from mid-April to the end of September (closed Saturdays early May to early July) and between 10am and 4pm from Sunday to Friday for the rest of the year (closed December 24th–26th and January 1st).

Bradenham Hall

Features an arboretum of more than 800 different, labelled species as well as fruit and vegetable gardens and herbaceous and mixed borders.

Castle Acre Priory & Castle

The Cluniac Priory here is thought to have evolved from an early monastery founded by William de Warenne, who came to England with William the Conqueror.

The remains, eight kilometres (five miles) north of Swaffham, give a glimpse of what was one of the most impressive 11th century priories in England.

Castle Acre's ruins span seven centuries and include a 12th century church, whose elaborately-decorated Great West Front still rises to its original height – a veritable masterpiece of Norman engineering.

There are also the remains of a 15th century gatehouse and a porch – as well as a Prior's lodging, which is still habitable.

Visitors can take a free audio tour and hear of the daily life of the monks as well as inspect the sites of the chapter house, cloister, dormitory and refectory.

Castle Acre Priory, which played a vital role in the life of the people in the area as the hub of a thriving community, is open daily between at least 10am and 5pm from April 1st to October 31st and between 10am and 4pm from November 1st to March 31st (Wednesday to Sunday only).

Parking, toilets and a shop are available at the site, where there is also a museum, gift shop and herb garden.

Cockley Cley Iceni Village & Museums

This unique interpretation of an Iceni village in the Iron Age includes a 17th century farm cottage and farm bygones, implements and carriages in a 200-year-old Norfolk barn.

The site also features the remains of St Mary's Chapel, a Saxon place of worship built in 630 AD.

Visitors can enjoy the nature trail, the lake and a bird-watching hide and can either take along a picnic or eat in the tearoom.

For children there are attractions such as a snake pit, face painting, a hanging skeleton and stocks.

The village and museums are open daily between at least 11am and 5pm from the beginning of April to the end of October.

Gooderstone Water Gardens

Gooderstone has three hectares (7½ acres) of gardens, herbaceous and water plants, a nature walk, roses, shrubs, rivers and a lake.

The gardens are open daily from the beginning of April to the end of October.

Narborough Trout Lakes

The lakes are part of a working trout farm providing stock for sporting fisheries as well as fresh or smoked trout for commercial or private customers.

Narborough, which has a picnic area and shop, also offers both novice and experienced anglers some challenging sport in either lake or stream.

Fly fishing lessons are available at both beginners' or advanced levels.

Oxburgh Hall

This beautiful moated manor house, 11 kilometres (seven miles) south-west of Swaffham, was built in 1482 by the Bedingfeld family, who are still residents.

It has a magnificent Tudor gatehouse and interesting private chapel and is surrounded by lovely

Cockley Cley Iceni Village

gardens, including a parterre, and woodland walks.

Inside the main house there is a display of tapestry and embroidery worked by Mary Queen of Scots during her captivity as well as a 16th century priest's hole and an armoury.

Captain Mainwaring, Sergeant Wilson and Corporal Pike feature in Oxburgh's more recent history – the Hall was a location for television's Dad's Army.

Croquet is among a number of special events organised at the hall.

The house is open daily (except for Mondays other than Bank Holidays, Thursdays and Fridays) between 1pm and 5pm from April 1st–26th and October 1st–29th; daily (except Thursdays and Fridays) from April 29th–July 31st and September 1st–30th; and daily in August.

The gardens can be visited between at least 11am and 4pm on Saturdays and Sundays from March 4th–26th; daily (except Thursdays and Fridays) from April 1st–July 31st and September 1st–October 29th; and daily throughout August.

There is a licensed restaurant open in the Old Kitchen between 11am and 5pm on the same days as the gardens and both Braille and children's guides are available.

Westacre Arts

West Acre, north west of Swaffham, is home to the celebrated Westacre Open Air arts season, which takes place in the West Acre Priory ruins.

Stephen Fry is a patron and activities were expanded in 2000 with the conversion of the old Methodist Chapel into the new River Studios.

Westacre performances have ranged from drama and comedy to choral, jazz and blues, while creative workshops have included writing, Greek drama and Shakespeare.

The 2000 season of events ran from early May to the end of July.

West Acre Gardens

This attraction, comprising a specialist plant nursery with display gardens, is just 5 kilometres (3 miles)

off the Peddars Way trail.

The gardens include many rarely-seen plants and many of these are propagated.

There are also mixed borders, specimen shrubs and trees, herbaceous perennials, ornamental grasses, alpines, roses and bamboos, a Mediterranean bed and a shade garden.

The gardens are open daily between 10am and 5pm from February to November.

Oxburgh Hall

EcoTech
Tel. 01760 726100
Fax. 01760 726109
e-mail:
info@ecotech.mplc.co.uk
web: www.ecotech.org.uk

Bradenham Hall
Tel. 01362 687243

Castle Acre Priory
Tel. 01760 755394

Cockley Cley Iceni Village
Tel. 01760 721339 or
724588

Gooderstone Water Gardens
Tel. 01366 328646

Narborough Trout Lakes
Tel. 01760 338005

Oxburgh Hall
Tel. 01366 328258
Fax. 01366 328066
e-mail:
aohusr@smtp.ntrust.org.uk

West Acre Arts (Box office)
Tel. 01760 755800

West Acre Gardens
Tel. 01760 755562

Norfolk Broads

The Norfolk Broads consist of around 200 kilometres (125 miles) of waterways formed in medieval times when peat was dug out for use as fuel in heating and cooking.

Some of the broads are surrounded by fens, consisting of reed and sedge, which are still cut for use in thatching.

Management of the reed beds sustains a perfect habitat for the rare and secretive bittern and creates ideal conditions for milk parsley on which the exquisite swallowtail butterfly feeds. Broadland is the only place in Britain where the swallowtail can still be seen.

Although first proposed as a National Park in 1947, The Broads were only eventually awarded comparable status in 1988 through the Norfolk & Suffolk Broads Act.

The River Ant at How Hill

Tourist Information Centres

Beccles (Seasonal)
Tel./Fax. 01502 713196

Great Yarmouth
Tel. 01493 846347; Fax. 01493 846221
e-mail: tourism@great-yarmouth.gov.uk

Hoveton (Seasonal)
Tel./Fax. 01603 782281

Lowestoft
Tel. 01502 523000; Fax. 01502 539023
e-mail: touristinfo@waveny.gov.uk

Norwich
Tel. 01603 666071; Fax. 01603 765389
e-mail: tourism.norwich@gtnet.gov.uk

Broads Authority Information Centres

(All Seasonal – Winter inquiries to Broads Authority)
Beccles Tel./Fax. 01502 713196
Great Yarmouth Tel./Fax. 01493 332095
Hoveton Tel./Fax. 01603 782281
How Hill Tel./Fax. 01692 678763
Loddon Tel. 01508 521028
Potter Heigham Tel./Fax. 01692 670779
Ranworth Tel./Fax. 01603 270453

Other Broads Information Centres

Stalham Staithe (Museum of the Broads) Tel. 01692 581681

Broads Authority

Tel. 01603 610734; Fax. 01603 765710
e-mail: broads-authority.gov.uk

Ordnance Survey Maps

OS Landranger sheet number 134; OS Outdoor Leisure sheet number 40

Great Yarmouth Area

Anyone wishing to step out of the comparative peace and tranquillity of Broadland into the highly-commercialised atmosphere of a busy seaside holiday resort will find plenty to keep them occupied in Great Yarmouth.

There's a large-scale **Pleasure Beach** for all the family on the sea front with over 20 large rides – including the Ejector Seat on which willing victims are hurled 49 metres (160 feet) into the air at 113 kilometres (70 miles) per hour!

The Pleasure Beach is open daily from the beginning of May to the beginning of September and at various other times out of the season.

Britannia Pier and Theatre at Marine Parade offers amusements, a funfair, restaurants and sideshows as well as top stars on stage in Summer.

There's also a **Marina Centre** with pool, **Model Village** and **Sealife Centre** on the seafront as well as a Louis Tussaud's **House of Wax** in Regent Road.

Away from the sea front, on the historic South Quay, there's **Elizabethan House Museum,** a Georgian fronted house now owned by the National Trust and managed by Norfolk Museums Service.

Just back from South Quay, there is also the **Tolhouse Museum** – complete with dungeons – in Yarmouth's former courtroom and goal and a **Maritime Museum** in a former home for shipwrecked sailors.

Berney Arms Windmill

One of the largest and best-preserved Victorian windmills in Norfolk with seven floors to explore, fully operational machinery and views over Breydon Water, Burgh Castle and the RSPB Halvergate reserve.

The Mill, preserved by English Heritage, is open daily between 9am to 1pm and 2–5pm from the beginning of April to the end of October.

Berney Marshes

This 364 hectare (900 acre) RSPB grassland reserve which can be found within the Halvergate grazing marshes and is accessible by public footpath or boat from Berney Arms.

The site, which features a picnic area, supports breeding wading birds such as lapwing, redshank and snipe.

There is a viewing screen and platform which overlooks pools used by roosting and feeding birds such as wigeon, golden plover and Bewick's swan in Winter, when the reserve is visited by a large flock of wintering wading birds as well as geese and wildfowl.

Breydon Water

The RSPB runs boat trips to see the geese, ducks and waders on Breydon on the first Sunday of every month.

Burgh Castle

The remains of a Roman fort, which defended the coast against Saxon invaders in the 3rd century.

The fort, which is to be found at the edge of the River Waveney, offers views over Breydon Water and Halvergate Marshes and is open daily.

Caister Castle

Motor museum in the grounds of a ruined 15th century castle, consisting of walls around a 30 metre (98ft) tower.

It is open daily, except Saturdays, between 10am and 4.30pm from mid-May to the end of September.

Fritton Lake Countryworld

Fritton Lake offers visitors the chance to go boating on one of the most beautiful stretches of water in East Anglia and explore just over 100 hectares (250 acres) of gardens and woodland.

The lake itself extends 3.6 kilometres (2¼ miles) from end to end, covers just over 60 hectares (150 acres) and has a miniature railway running along a half-mile track beside it.

There are rowing boats or pedalos to hire or an electrically-powered

Great Yarmouth Pleasure Beach

Pleasure Beach
Tel. 01493 844585

Britannia Pier
administration
Tel. 01493 842914
box office
Tel. 01493 842209

Marina Centre
Tel. 01493 851521
Fax. 01493 330852

Model Village
Tel. 01493 842097

Sea Life Centre
Tel. 01493 330631

House of Wax
Tel. 01493 844851

Elizabethan House
Tel. 01493 855746

Tolhouse Museum
Tel. 01493 858900

Maritime Museum
Tel. 01493 842267

Museums Office
Tel. 01493 745526

Berney Arms Windmill
Tel. 01493 700605
web: www.english-heritage.org.uk

Berney Marshes RSPB
Tel. 01493 700645

**Breydon Water RSPB
boat trips**
Tel. 01603 715191 or 01493 700645

Caister Castle
Tel. 01572 787251

Fritton Lake Countryworld
Tel. 01493 488208

boat operates guided tours.

The cost of playing Fritton's 9-hole golf course and 18-hole putting green is included in the entrance charge.

There's an adventure playground, including assault course and aerial slides, for children and a children's farm gives them the chance to meet a

☎ FAX 💻

Great Yarmouth Racecourse
Tel. 01493 842527
Fax. 01493 843254

Horsey Windpump (NT)
Tel. 01493 393904

Pettitts Animal Adventure Park
information line
Tel. 01493 700094 or 701403
Fax. 01493 700933
web: www.pettitts.com

Raveningham Hall
Tel. 01508 548206

Thrigby Hall Wildlife Gardens
Tel. 01493 369477

Village Experience
Tel. 0870 5134890
e-mail: office@thevillage-experience.com
web: www.thevillage-experience.com

variety of animals and drive a battery-powered miniature tractor.

Wagon and pony rides operate from the Heavy Horse Centre and throughout the Summer birds of prey including hawks, falcons, kites, vultures, buzzards, owls and eagles give flying displays.

Fritton Lake is open daily between 10am and 5.30pm from the beginning of April almost to the end of September as well as at week-ends only and half-term week in October.

Golf and fishing only are available throughout the Winter.

Great Yarmouth Races

Many top owners, trainers and jockeys visit the course at Jellicoe Road, Great Yarmouth, during the season, which opens at the end of May.

Facilities include two restaurants and a fast food court.

Horsey Windpump

Near Horsey village is this early 20th century drainage windpump, which is open daily between 11am and 5pm from the beginning of April to the end of September and offers good views from the top.

There is also a marked circular walk from the car park and access to the beach at Horsey Gap car park as well as a National Trust shop at Horsey Staithe stores.

Pettitts Animal Adventure Park

A family park with special appeal for children and adults.

There are animals galore, including birds of prey, chickens, ducks, miniature Fallabella horses, goats, monkeys, parrots, peacocks, rhea and wallabies as well as an adventure play area and a wide variety of rides and shows.

Pettitts is also widely known for its flower feathercraft and

various arrangements and designs can be seen being made or on display in the showrooms.

Raveningham Hall

Raveningham is a 19th century house with a commercial nursery including rare shrubs and herbaceous plants, a conservatory and walled kitchen garden.

The grounds were laid out at the beginning of the century but several new areas have been designed and added over the last 30 years.

Raveningham, 15 kilometres (nine miles) south west of Great Yarmouth off the B1136, is open between 2pm and 5pm on Sundays and Bank Holiday Mondays in May, June and July as well as Easter Sunday and Monday.

Thrigby Hall Wildlife Gardens

A collection of wildlife from many parts of Asia set in acres of the Norfolk countryside at Filby, near Great Yarmouth.

Thrigby, which features a free car park, children's play area, picnic areas, café and gift shop, is open daily from 10am.

The Village Experience

This visitor attraction at Fleggburgh, between Acle and Caister, is a 12-hectare (30-acre) woodland attraction which includes working steam, fairground rides including Victorian Gallopers, puppets and live shows.

There are also bygones and memorabilia, a drawing and painting studio for children, farm animals, crafts and shops, an indoor soft play area, a junior maze and train rides.

In the Exploratorium, full of the weird and the wonderful, there is the opportunity to shake hands with yourself, make shadows and watch time tick by.

Another feature, Dancing waters, continues an old tradition of making the movements of water match the rhythms of music.

The Village is open daily from the week prior to Easter to the last Sunday in October between 10am and 5pm.

Pettitts Animal Adventure Park

Norwich Cathedral

Norwich Area

Broads cruisers – and even much larger vessels – can sail right into the heart of this East Anglian capital city and moor up at the **Yacht Station** with a view of the **Cathedral** across the fields.

This famous Norwich landmark, with a 96-metre (315-ft) steeple second in height only to that of Salisbury, was the vision of the first Bishop of Norwich, Herbert de Losinga.

Built of limestone from Caen in Normandy, it was begun in 1096 but was not finally consecrated until 1278.

With East Anglia isolated by marshes and fenland in medieval times, for centuries the river was the city's lifeblood – and one of its few direct trading links with the outside world.

Today the Wensum is enjoyed for leisure purposes. Boats venture as far downstream as Surlingham Broad and a city centre riverside walk allows pedestrians to follow the river in peaceful surroundings.

Another river, the Yare passes through countryside to the south and west of Norwich.

The city is connected to the rest of the Broads system by the two rivers and to the south east there is the recently-established Whitlingham Little Broad where

canoeing, sailing and windsurfing take place in Summer.

Visitors to Norwich itself can enjoy a wide range of amenities and attractions, apart from the Cathedral – from the similarly Norman castle to the ultra-modern **Castle Mall shopping Centre** just a stone's throw away.

There is a market place where stalls do a thriving business, a magnificent timber-framed merchant's building in **The Dragon Hall** plus museums which include the **castle** itself (closed for improvements until Spring 2001), the **Bridewell** in Bridewell Alley and the famous Colman's **Mustard Shop** in the late 19th century Royal Arcade.

Other favourite haunts for visitors are Elm Hill, a cobbled and carefully-preserved medieval street, and the Georgian **Assembly House** – sensitively restored after being gutted by fire in 1995.

Even the Tourist Information Centre for the city is housed in an historic building – the medieval Guildhall, on the north side of the market square.

Ranworth Area

Fairhaven Woodland and Water Garden

This beautiful South Walsham property consists of 73 hectares (180 acres) of ancient woodland, water gardens and a private broad, all environmentally managed.

The garden was left in trust by the second Lord Fairhaven in 1973, opened to the public in 1975 and celebrated its 25th Anniversary on April 18th 2000.

Over 90 species of birds have been recorded at Fairhaven during the seasons and the three native woodpeckers – Greater Spotted, Lesser Spotted and Green – are resident.

Special features in the grounds include a 950-year-old King Oak tree, a water trail (which can be explored

Fairhaven Woodland and Water Garden

by boat from April to the end of October at an additional cost) and a children's nature trail.

Fairhaven, which features a tearoom, gift shop and plant sales areas, is open daily (except Christmas Day) all year round from 10am

☎ FAX 🖵

Yacht Station
Tel. 01603 622024

Cathedral
Tel. 01603 764385/ 767617
Fax. 01603 766032

Castle Mall Shopping Centre
Tel. 01603 766430
Fax. 01603 766917

Dragon Hall
Tel. 01603 663922

Castle Museum (Closed until Spring 2001)
Tel. 01603 493624
Fax. 01603 765651

Bridewell Museum
Tel. 01603 667228

Mustard Shop
Tel. 01603 627889
Fax. 01603 762142

Assembly House
Tel. 01603 626402
Fax. 01603 632468

Fairhaven Woodland and Water Garden
Tel./Fax. 01603 270449
web: www.norfolkbroads.com/fairhaven

Arthur Ransome boats Nancy Blackett (left) and Peter Duck – see 'The Coot Club' (below)

to 5pm Closing time is extended to 9pm on Wednesday and Thursday evenings from May until the end of August.

Special events include a number of guided walks.

Ranworth Broad Wildlife Centre

Ranworth Broad, part of the Bure Marshes National Nature Reserve, is close to the River Bure and the village of Ranworth.

A boardwalk trail leads through woodland and reedbed to the broad and the thatched floating conservation centre, which offers interactive displays and excellent views over the open water.

Afloat in Broadland

Broads Wherries

The heyday of the trading wherry was in the 19th century, when several hundred sailed the Broadland waterways.

The advent of the railways and motor transport gradually led to their demise, however, and by 1945 there were none left trading under sail.

When The Broads were 'discovered' as a holiday destination in the mid-19th century, enterprising wherry owners would convert the interior of their vessel to accommodate holidaymakers during the season and then revert back to trading.

By the 1880s purpose-built pleasure wherries were being built, with crisp, white sails replacing the tar and herring oil-coated black sails of the traders.

Canoe Hire

New for the year 2000 was a Broads Authority canoe hire initiative, offering from five centres full or half-day hire (including buoyancy aids) of 'Canadian' two and three-seater canoes suitable for all the family.

The canoes can be hired from Bungay (Outney Meadows Caravan Park – Tel. 01986 892338), Horstead near Coltishall (Norfolk School of Canoeing – Tel. 01603 737456), Norwich (City Boats, Riverside Road – Tel. 01603 701701), Sutton Staithe (Sutton Staithe Boatyard – Tel. 01692 5816532) and Wayford Bridge (Bank Dayboats – Tel. 01692 582071).

Norfolk Wherry Trust

Perhaps the best-known Wherry to be seen in Broadland for many years has been the Albion – last of the Black-sailed traders – who celebrated her centenary in 1998.

Known at one time as the Plane, she was bought by the then newly-formed Norfolk Wherry Trust in 1949 and restored at a cost of £1033.

By October the following year she had sailed more than 3218 kilometres (2000 miles) with cargo but by 1961 it had been decided that she would carry only people.

Up to 12 can sail on Albion with an experienced skipper and mate and she can be chartered for a day's cruise – or longer voyages, as she is equipped with bunks.

Information about membership of the Norfolk Wherry Trust can be obtained from John Cooper at 20 Latchmoore Park, Ludham, Norfolk NR29 5RA.

The Coot Club

Visitors familiar with the books of Arthur Ransome will be aware that two of them – The Coot Club and Big Six – were set on the Norfolk Broads.

Ransome first visited the Broads in 1919 and spent sailing holidays in the area twice in the early Thirties.

With the idea of a book set on the Broads in mind, he returned in 1934 and cruised to all the places subsequently featured in The Coot Club, taking photographs of them as well.

The book features an incident when the Death and Glories catch a large pike – and this was probably inspired by a 9.5kg (21lb) fish displayed at the Swan Inn at Horning.

Some of the craft featured in the two books are now being restored at the Museum of the Broads at Stalham (q.v.).

Guided boat trips operate for an additional cost at certain times and special events include a two-hour batwatch which is organised by the Norfolk Wildlife Trust and starts at the Visitor Centre.

Car parking is in the village for Ranworth as there is no car park at the reserve entrance. Following signs from the staithe, it is a five minute walk to the reserve.

The nearby 14th century **St Helen's Church,** known as 'The Cathedral of the Broads' is worth a visit – not only for the wonderful view of the reserve it offers from the top of its 29 metre (90 ft) tower but also for its famous painted rood screen.

In fact a ghostly monk is said to row across the Broad on dark nights to complete the task of restoration he began on the screen in the 16th century.

Ranworth reserve is open all year and the conservation centre between 10am and 5pm from April and October. No dogs are allowed on the reserve.

An information leaflet on Ranworth – where booking is essential for group visits – is available from the Norfolk Wildlife Trust.

Stalham Area

Hickling Broad

Hickling, largest of the Norfolk Broads, is a national nature reserve and home to some of the rarest plants and animals – including the bittern and swallowtail butterfly.

There is a car park, hides, picnic site, visitor centre, three signed circular walks (guide dogs only) and wildlife gift shop.

An elevated observation hut offers visitors spectacular views across the reserve, where bearded tits, kingfishers, marsh harriers, redshank, various wading birds, dragonflies and even red deer can be seen.

Guided walks and information leaflets are available at the visitor centre together with details of the guided boat trail (booking essential), which operates from the Pleasure

Boat Inn at Hickling Staithe most days between June and September.

The staff at Hickling offer a range of education activities and guided walks for schools and other groups.

The Hickling reserve, six kilometres (four miles) south of the market town of Stalham on the upper reaches of the River Thurne, is open all year round and the visitor centre from 10am to 5pm daily from April to September.

How Hill, Ludham, and Wildlife Water Trail

How Hill, north west of Ludham on the River Ant, was opened to visitors some 14 years ago – having previously been a county council educational study centre and a private property.

The reserve and nature trail are now managed by the Broads Authority, which also looks after the small Toad Hole Cottage museum, housed in a former marshman's home and open daily between 10 am and 6 pm from June to September and between 11 am and 5 pm from Easter to May as well as in October.

The **'Electric Eel',** which operates from the staithe at How Hill and tours the reeds and fen of nearby dykes and rivers, is an Edwardian-style boat seating some eight people.

The 'Eel's' 50-minute trip includes a stop at a landing stage and a visit to a nearby hide, to look at the bird life attracted to a flooded marshland area.

The Staithe at How Hill

Ranworth Broad Wildlife Centre (NWT)
Tel. 01603 270479

St Helen's Church & Visitor Centre
Tel. 01603 270511

Hickling Broad National Nature Reserve (NWT)
Tel. 01692 598276

How Hill (Electric Eel Booking Line)
Tel. 01692 678763

Norfolk Wherry Trust
Tel. 01953 850181

How Hill, which also has a walking wildlife trail (open at the same times as the water trail) is off the A1062 Wroxham to Potter Heigham road – look for signposts.

There is a free public car park on the left as you approach from Ludham and free public mooring near the thatched boat shed at the staithe.

Walk slightly downhill across the Fisherman's Field to find Toad Hole Cottage which issues tickets for the Electric Eel boat trips departing from the public staithe near the thatched boat shed.

The Electric Eel runs on the hour, every hour, between 11am and 3pm at weekends, Bank Holidays and local half term from Easter to May and during October. From June to September trips operate daily between 10am and 5pm.

Tickets can be obtained from Toad Hole Cottage or from Broads Information Centres.

Hickling Broad

Museum of the Broads, Stalham Staithe

Museum of the Broads

An exhibition of Broads history and boat design through the ages which started life at Potter Heigham but moved to historic old buildings at Stalham Staithe in 1999 and is still developing.

Exhibits include a period River Commissioner's launch, a steam launch, gun punts – and the only concrete dinghy ever constructed!

The museum is open between 11am and 5pm from Easter to October and special events, displays and demonstrations are held throughout the season.

Potter Heigham

Broadland village with a low bridge notorious for catching out unwary boating Broads holidaymakers.

Solar-Powered Boat Trips

From Easter 2001 onwards the Broads Authority is offering trips around Barton Broad on the Ra – a £55,000 German-built, solar-powered boat unveiled at How Hill in September 2000.

The 30 ft boat, named after the Egyptian sun god, has three rows of solar panels and can carry 12 people at a time.

Stalham Water Tours

River tours (with commentary) operated from Richardson's Boatyard in a 50-seater all-weather luxury cruiser – MC Osprey – between Easter and the end of September.

A 1½ hour tour makes for Barton Broad via Hunsett Mill and Barton Turf, while a 2¾ hour cruise to

Walks and Tours

Broadland By Car, By Cycle or On Foot

Broadland District Council's Leisure and Tourism Department at Thorpe Lodge, 1 Yarmouth Road, Thorpe St Andrew, Norwich NR7 0DU (Tel. 01603 431133; Fax. 300087) can supply leaflets on a number of quiet walks and 'Off The Beaten Track' car tours and cycle tours which can be enjoyed in the area as well as on Broadland's churches and market towns.

Walks cover the Bure Valley, Foulsham, Halvergate, Horsford and St Faiths Common, Marriotts Way, Reepham, Ringland and Swannington.

Cycle tours are around the Blofield, Drayton, Reepham, Ringland and Swannington areas and car tours from Blickling to Cawston, Great Plumstead to Acle and Horsham St Faith to Aylsham.

Eight circular Broads bike trails feature in leaflets and maps published by the Broads Authority and available at 20 pence each or £1 for the set from Broads Information Centres and the Broads Authority offices at 18, Colegate, Norwich NR3 1BQ.

There are also seven other leaflets, each covering a longer trail, available at 25 pence each or £1.50 for the set.

Ten Bike Hire points are listed in a separate free Broads Authority leaflet, although this does not include maps (Further details from Broads Information line on 01603 782281).

The bike points are at Acle Bridge (Bridge Stores – Tel. 01493 730355), Bungay (Outney Meadow Caravan Park – Tel. 01986 892338), Hickling (Pleasure Boat Stores – Tel. 07747 066606), Hoveton (Camelot Craft or Bure Valley Railway – Tel. 01603 783096 for both), Loddon (Broadland Riverine Boatcraft – Tel. 01508 528735), Ludham (Ludham Bridge Boat Services – Tel. 01692 630486), Neatishead (Barton Angler Inn – Tel. 01692 630740), Norwich (City Boats, Yacht Station and Highcraft, Thorpe – Tel. 01603 701701 for both), Sutton Staithe (Sutton Staithe Boatyard – Tel. 01692 581653) and Thurne Staithe (Thurne Stores – Tel. 01493 369235).

Barton Broad and the River Ant includes a conducted tour of the gardens at How Hill.

Sutton Windmill

Although no longer working, this Norfolk landmark has nine floors and is claimed to be the tallest British windmill still standing.

The derelict corn mill, built over 200 years ago and in use until 1940, was bought a few years ago by Chris Nunn and his family, who began the still-continuing restoration work.

There is a remarkable view from the top of the building – reached by nine steep ladders – and at the bottom a remarkable **museum of social life** developed from the Nunn family's private collection.

The Mill is open daily between 10am and 5.30pm from April 1st to September 30th.

Wroxham Area

Barton House Railway

A 7¼-inch gauge line which operates two railways and steam rides in gardens on the edge of the River Bure.

The railway, at Hartwell Road, Wroxham, is open only between 2.30pm and 5.30pm on the third Sunday in the month from April to October.

Access to the site is by road, boat or electric ferry from Wroxham Bridge.

Broads Tours

Hires out an electric picnic day boat and electric or diesel self-drive day boats seating between six and eight people.

The company also offers river trips with commentary on double-decker or traditional cruisers from its bases at Wroxham bridge and Potter Heigham bridge.

Hoveton Hall Gardens

Grounds which include 4 hectares (10 acres) of rhododendron and azalea-filled woodland as well as formal herbaceous borders and a lakeside walk.

The gardens are open between 11am and 5.30pm on two Sundays in April and then on Wednesdays, Fridays, Sundays and Bank Holiday Mondays from Easter until almost the end of September.

Mississippi Paddle Boat

A hundred-seater, double-decker riverboat, The Southern Comfort, operates daily 60-minute or 90-minute trips with commentary from a mooring near the Swan Hotel at Horning between May and September.

Norfolk Broads Yachting Company at Horning

Runs largest hire fleet of sailing yachts on Norfolk Broads.

White Moth, which sleeps up to 10 passengers, is a gaff-rigged Edwardian wherry yacht – one of only three of its type left – and comes complete with a skipper and local guide, who have separate crew quarters.

St Benet's Abbey

St Benet's Abbey

Remains, on the banks of the River Bure, of what was, before the Norman conquest, the only religious building in Norfolk.

Bishops of Norwich have remained Abbots to the present time and, arriving by wherry, preach at the site on the first Sunday in August each year.

Wherry Yacht Charter

This Wroxham-based company operates Harthor, which is now the only Broads pleasure wherry still available for charter.

It also owns two wherry yachts – Olive, which sleeps up to 11 passengers, and Norada, which sleeps 10 – similarly available for hire throughout the year.

For the 2000 season, the Broads Authority chartered all three vessels – complete with skippers and crew – so as to offer holidaymakers the chance to enjoy short trips, half-days or full days on a wherry.

Wroxham Barns

This restored 18th century barn complex at Tunstead Road, Hoveton, some 16 kilometres (ten miles) north-east of Norwich, features 12 working craftsmen, a junior farm, traditional fair, tea-rooms, craft and gift shop, gallery and clothing collection.

Weather permitting, the fair operates between 11am to 5pm from Easter to early September.

The Junior Farm – where there are chickens, cows, donkeys, goats, guinea pigs, lambs, pigs and rabbits which can be handled and fed by children – is open from the beginning of May to the beginning of September.

When there are lambs, they are fed at 11am, 1.30pm and 3.30pm.

The Norfolk Cider Company – established 13 years ago and one of only about a dozen traditional cider makers left in the East of England – can also be found at the family leisure centre.

Wroxham Barns is open free with

A Broads wherry

Museum of the Broads
Tel. 01692 581681
e-mail: museum@whiteswan.co.uk

Solar-Powered Boat Trips
Tel. 01692 678763

Stalham Water Tours
Tel. 01692 670530

Sutton Windmill and Broads Museum
Tel./Fax. 01692 581195

Broads Tours
Tel. 01603 782207

Hoveton Hall Gardens
Tel. 01603 782798

Mississippi River Boat
Tel. 01692 630262

Norfolk Broads Yachting Company
Tel. 01692 631330
web: www.nbyco.com

Wherry Yacht Charter
Tel. 01603 782470

Wroxham Barns
Tel. 01603 783762
Fax. 01603 781401
information line
Tel. 01603 783911

free car parking from 10am to 5pm all year round, with the exception of Christmas and New Year.

There are facilities for disabled visitors (guide dogs only are allowed on site) and advance bookings for coach parties and groups are welcome.

North Suffolk

An area which combines historic towns and villages with quaint harbours, award-winning sandy beaches and leisure pursuits in abundance.

Lowestoft, which once boasted an impressive herring fishing industry, and Oulton Broad with its waterside park are both popular holiday resorts.

To the south, meanwhile, the ancient Borough of Southwold – home to the celebrated Adnams brewery – offers Georgian charm and a chance to step back in time, away from the hurly-burly of modern life.

Across the River Blyth, Walberswick is the haunt of painters past and present – and the home of the annual charity fund-raising British Open Crabbing Championship.

Famous names connected with the area include Charles Dickens, who visited Blundeston, north of Lowestoft, and is said to have used the Rectory and the Plough Inn as part of the setting for David Copperfield.

Tourist Information Centres

Beccles (Easter to October)
Tel./Fax. 01502 713196

Lowestoft
Tel. 01502 533600; Fax. 01502 539023
e-mail: touristinfo@waveney.gov.uk
web: www.visit-lowestoft.co.uk

Southwold
Tel. 01502 724729; Fax. 01502 722978
e-mail: southwold.tic@waveney.gov.uk
web: www.visit-southwold.co.uk

Ordnance Survey Maps

OS Landranger sheet numbers: 134, 156

Southwold Lighthouse

Beccles

Beccles Museum

This museum at Ballygate, Beccles, features local history – including the printing industry for which the area was particularly known in the past.

There's a 19th century printing press on show as well as exhibits of agricultural and domestic items and items concerned with the natural history of the river.

The museum is open between 2.30pm and 5pm from Tuesday to Sunday each week (as well as on Bank Holidays) from Easter to October.

William Clowes Print Museum

Located at Newgate, Beccles, the museum – which covers the development of the printing industry in Beccles from 1800 – is open between 2pm and 4pm Monday to Friday from June to August.

Guided tours are available by arrangement.

Beccles Area

Waveney Rush Industry

Waveney Rush, based at Aldeby, near Beccles, is, perhaps strangely, part of the Waveney Apple Growers group.

Rush weaving, referred to by Chaucer in the Canterbury Tales, dates back to early Anglo Saxon days and grew from the custom of rushes being strewn loosely as a floor covering.

Waveney Rush have been making rush matting since 1947 and their work can still be seen in many

The Otter Trust, Earsham

National Trust properties, churches and museums.

The company also makes coasters, mats, deck shoe baskets and cat and dog baskets.

Bungay

Bungay Castle

Remains, in the centre of Bungay, of a Norman castle built by the Bigod family in 1165.

The castle, which features twin towers and massive flint walls, is open between 9am and 5pm from Monday to Saturday and 10am and 2pm on Sundays.

A notice board at the site specifies nearby premises from which keys to the keep are available.

Bungay Museum

Housed in the Waveney District Council offices at Broad Street, Bungay, and covering local history, including coins, pictures and a model of Bungay Castle.

Open between 9am and 1pm and 2–4 pm from Monday to Friday all year round (closed Bank Holidays).

Bungay Area

The Cider Place

This small family establishment at Ilketshall St Lawrence, midway between Bungay and Halesworth, offers visitors the chance to see traditional apple pressing equipment at work – and taste the results.

The Cider Place is open daily (except for Wednesdays and Sunday mornings) all year round between 9am and 1pm and 2–6pm and admission is free.

Otter Trust

The headquarters of the Trust, just off the A143 Harleston to Bungay road at Earsham, near Bungay, are open between 10.30am and 6pm from the beginning of April to the end of October.

Waveney Rush Industry, Aldeby

Beccles Museum
Tel. 01502 715722

William Clowes Print Museum
Tel. 01502 712884

Waveney Rush Industry
Tel. 01502 538777
Fax. 01502 538477
e-mail: crafts@ waveneyrush.co.uk
web: www. waveneyrush.co.uk

Bungay Museum
Tel. 01986 892176

Cider Place
Tel. 01986 781353

Otter Trust
Tel. 01986 893470
web: ottertrust.org.uk/ earsham.htm

Apart from British and Asian otters, the riverside premises also feature small Muntjac deer, a breeding colony of night herons, red-necked wallabies and a variety of waterfowl.

Otter numbers in the wild have declined dramatically over the years as a result of modern farming methods – particularly the use of pesticides and other chemicals.

By the early eighties, the creatures were coming close to extinction in East Anglia.

Now, however, thanks to the Trust's reintroduction programme – begun in 1983 and carried out with the co-operation of English Nature and the County Naturalists Trusts – the regional population has been restored to that of 20 years ago.

South Elmham Hall Farm

Once a hunting palace for the Bishop of Norwich – who kept a large deer park – this 182 hectare (450 acre) arable farm with its 13th century hall standing in a 1.6 hectare (4 acre) moated site won a conservation prize in 1997.

A network of five different walks, of varying length, cut through the historic landscape – which includes an 11th century Saxon ruin, known as The Minster, and 11 kilometres (seven miles) of hedgerow.

Wildlife attracted to the area includes hares, herons, woodpeckers, snipe and sandpipers and three species of owls while, during the Winter, teal and golden plovers can sometimes be seen.

The farm also supports a small herd of relatively rare British White cattle, an ancient breed traditionally kept in parks or by religious orders.

As well as opening the walks to the public (who are not charged but are invited to make donations via a box on

St Peter's Hall, St Peter South Elmham

the free car park) the hall offers bed and breakfast accommodation.

St Peter's Hall & Brewery

St Peter's is located in an area near Bungay called 'The Saints' – because almost every village there is named after one of them.

The hall, at St Peter South Elmham, dates from around 1280 but was extended in 1539, using 14th Century 'architectural salvage' taken from Flixton Priory.

The surrounding moat dates from the 11th or 12th Century and was stocked with fish – mainly mirror carp – in 1997.

Although brewing has been practised at the site for a thousand years, the brewery (housed in listed former agricultural buildings) is quite a recent addition, having been built in 1996.

The site was chosen because there is a deep borehole within a chalk layer way below St Peter's Hall and the water – softened by the chalk layers through which it is drawn – is ideal for brewing.

St Peters produces 'real ale' and has a normal capacity of 300 barrels or almost 400,000 litres (86,000 pints) a week – though its comfortable capacity is less than half of that.

Its range of brews includes Fruit Beer (elderberry or grapefruit),

Wheat Beer, Lemon and Ginger Spiced Ale, Old Style Porter, Strong Ale, Winter Ale, Suffolk Gold (with all Suffolk grown hops and barley malt) Spiced Ale, Summer Ale, Honey Porter, Golden Ale, Cream Stout and Organic Ale.

The hall is open as a bar and restaurant every Friday, Saturday and Sunday as well as on Bank Holiday Mondays.

Wingfield Old College and Gardens

A timber-framed medieval hall hidden behind an 18th century façade with walled gardens which include ancient ponds, topiary and statuary.

A season of concerts is held in either the college or the adjoining church and there are art exhibitions in the visitor centre.

Wingfield, which also provides home-made teas, is open between 2pm and 6pm on Saturdays, Sundays and Bank Holiday Mondays from Easter to September.

Lowestoft

East Point Pavilion

An impressive glass visitor centre, which is open daily and overlooks Lowestoft's award-winning sandy

South Elmham Hall Farm
Tel. 01986 782526
Fax. 01986 782203
e-mail: Jo.Sanderson@btinternet.com

St Peter's Hall & Brewery
Tel. 01986 782322
Fax. 01986 782505
e-mail: beers@stpetersbrewery.co.uk
web:
www.stpetersbrewery.co.uk

Wingfield Old College and Gardens
Tel. 01379 384888

East Point Pavilion
Tel. 01502 533600
Fax. 01502 539023

South Beach.

Built around 1993, the centre has been extensively renovated and now combines a tourist information centre with a restaurant and a multi-level 'Mayhem' adventure play area for children.

Flying Fifteens Tea Room

A good place to sample fresh fish in Lowestoft is the Flying Fifteens tearoom – named after the racing dinghy designed by Uffa Fox.

The upmarket establishment on Lowestoft's Esplanade is open from Easter to the end of September and was recently given an Award of Excellence by the British Tea Council after being secretly vetted on everything from the quality of its tea to the condition of the toilets.

International Sailing Craft Association's Maritime Museum

The ISCA is a registered charity which was established in 1969 and aims to preserve and restore sailing craft from around the world.

Its museum at Caldecott Road, Oulton Broad, Lowestoft, has possibly the largest internationally-recognised collection of craft with some 300 exhibits ranging from dinghies to dugouts to dhows and skiffs to sampans.

Some of the more exotic boats are occasionally displayed on Oulton Broad during the Summer months.

The museum is open every day (except Christmas Day and New Year's Day) between 10am and 6pm from April to October and 10am and 4pm from November to March (last admissions one hour before closing).

Facilities include free parking, access for the disabled, a small gift shop and evening visits by arrangement.

Kensington Gardens

Formal gardens set out at the top of the Esplanade with splendid views out to sea.

They include an aviary, bowling green, sunken garden, tennis courts and tearooms.

Lowestoft & East Suffolk Maritime Museum

Established in 1968 with the focus on Lowestoft and its fishing industry, this museum includes models of fishing and merchant ships as well as a lifeboat display.

It is open daily between 10am and 5pm from May to the end of September at Sparrows Nest Gardens, Whapload Road, Lowestoft.

Lowestoft Museum

Covers the history of the town from the Stone Age to the present.

Exhibits include geological items, kitchen utensils, a collection of Lowestoft porcelain, radios, Roman and medieval finds as well as a reconstruction of a cobbler's shop.

The museum is open at Nicholas Everitt Park, Oulton Broad, from 10.30am–1pm and 2–5pm between Monday and Saturday and on Sundays between 2pm and 5pm from mid-May to early October.

Also open Saturdays and Sundays between 2pm and 5pm from mid-April to mid-May and between 2pm and 4pm in October.

Lowestoft Seafront Air Festival

A two-day free festival which is held at the beginning of August each year and attracts some 200,000 spectators.

Open from 10am to 10pm each day, it includes everything from the three-hour continuous flying displays themselves (between 2pm and 5pm) to flight simulators, funfair rides, jazz bands, stalls, street entertainers and fireworks finales.

Advance programmes are usually available from the East Point Pavilion Visitor Centre at Royal Plain from the first week in July.

Lowestoft War Museum

Housed at Sparrow's Nest, in the north of the

Flying Fifteens Tea Room
Tel. 01502 581188

ISCA Maritime Museum
Tel. 01502 585606
Fax. 01502 589014
e-mail:
isca.maritimemuseum@
btinternet.com
web: www.btinternet.com/
~isca.maritimemuseum

Lowestoft & East Suffolk Maritime Museum
Tel. 01502 561963

Lowestoft Museum
Tel. 01502 511457 or 572811

Lydia Eva and Mincarlo Charitable Trust
Tel. 01502 560992

town, and dedicated to everyone who served at Lowestoft during the Second World War.

Lydia Eva & Mincarlo

The fishing vessel Lydia Eva was built in 1930 and is a reminder of the East Coast's heyday of plentiful catches.

She is the sole survivor of the thousands of steam herring drifters which once thronged Lowestoft and Great Yarmouth.

Until 1938, the Lydia Eva worked the home herring fishery in the Autumn, trawled in the Summer – usually in the Irish Sea but occasion-

Lowestoft harbour

ally in the North Sea – and between times fished from other western ports.

Lydia Eva's benefactors now also maintain the last completely Lowestoft-built and engined mid-water 'Sidewinder' trawler, Mincarlo.

The two vessels alternate annually between berths near the Haven Bridge at Great Yarmouth and the Heritage Quay in Lowestoft Yacht Basin. (In 2000, Lydia Eva was at Yarmouth and Mincarlo was at Lowestoft).

Both are open to the public, from whom donations are welcome, between 10 am and 3.30 pm daily from Easter until the end of October.

☎ FAX 🖥

Lowestoft Marina Theatre (Box Office)
Tel. 01502 533200
Fax: 01502 538179
e-mail:
info@marinatheatre.co.uk
web:
www.marinatheatre.co.uk

Pakefield Riding School
Tel. 01502 572257
Fax: 01502 537635

Royal Naval Patrol Service Museum
Tel. 01502 564344

East Anglia Transport Museum
Tel. 01502 518459

East Anglia Transport Museum, Carlton Colville

Marina Theatre

This council-owned theatre in Lowestoft's Marina offers a wide range of popular programming – from comedy to music and plays – and organises a variety of workshops throughout the season.

Nicholas Everitt Park

Attractive waterside park at Oulton Broad, offering a variety of leisure pursuits and a front-row view of Thursday evening hydroplane and motor boat racing during the season.

Pakefield Riding School

Pakefield Riding School at Carlton Road, Lowestoft was established in 1946 and has been a member of the Riding for the Disabled Association for 35 years.

The school stables 30 horses, ranging from small ponies to heavy cobs, has a floodlit indoor riding school and jumping paddock and offers riding lessons for both able bodied and disabled students.

Royal Naval Patrol Service Museum

Contains reminders, through models, documents, photographs and certificates, of how a flotilla of small ships operating from Lowestoft during the Second World War kept the sea-lanes clear.

Open at Sparrows Nest from mid-May to early October between 10am and 12 noon and 2pm and 4.30pm (Monday to Friday) and 2pm and 4.30pm (Sunday).

Sparrow's Nest Gardens

Britain's most easterly park includes a bandstand, bar, bowling and putting greens, restaurant and tennis courts.

Pleasurewood Hills, Corton

Lowestoft Area

Benacre Broad

Benacre National Nature Reserve includes reedbeds, saline lagoons and the shingle beaches of Benacre and Covehithe, as well as woodlands and grass heath on the higher ground.

There are more than a hundred breeding species of birds, including marsh harrier, bearded reedling, water rail and a variety of ducks. Bittern use the area for feeding and sand martins can be seen from the beach.

The reed-bed is home to the very rare white-mantled wainscot moth, considered extinct in Britain for over 100 years – until it was discovered on this site.

The reserve is privately owned and access by public footpath is available across parts of the reserve. There is courtesy access along the beach with a short privilege route to the public hide on the south side of Benacre Broad.

NB. The cliffs here are very dangerous.

East Anglia Transport Museum

This museum at Chapel Road, Carlton Colville, near Lowestoft, features a collection of vintage cars and historic trams and trolleybuses.

It is the only place in Britain where visitors can not only view but also ride on all three principal forms of public transport from the earlier part of this century.

There is also a period street complete with authentic street furniture and the East Suffolk Light Railway winds its way around the site, which features a bookshop and tearooms.

The museum is open between 11am and 5.30pm on Sundays and Bank Holiday Mondays between 2pm and 5pm on Wednesdays and Saturdays from April to September and between 2pm and 5pm from mid-July until the end of August.

Pleasurewood Hills

Billed as 'East Anglia's Biggest Day Out', this American-style theme park can be found at Leisure Way, Corton, near Lowestoft.

The park is open on Saturdays and Sundays from mid-April as well as two weeks at the end of both April and May, daily throughout June, July and August and week-ends plus the odd full week in both September and October.

Admission prices include unlimited use of all main rides, shows and attractions with the exception of games, go-karts and coin-operated amusements.

Somerleyton Hall

Although it stands on the site of an earlier Jacobean manor house, Someleyton Hall, as seen today, is unmistakably Victorian.

The transformation was carried out between 1844 and 1851 by self-made entrepreneur, Norwich M.P. and then owner Sir Morton Peto, employing John Thomas – protégé of Sir Charles Barry and Prince Albert – as architect.

Primarily a sculptor and ornamental mason – he worked for 17 years on the Houses of Parliament – Thomas was also responsible for much of the rebuilding of St Mary's Church, Somerleyton, and the 35 romantic thatched cottages around the village green.

Surrounding the Hall – whose contents include an exquisite silver and gilt moulded mirror made

originally for the Doge's Palace in Venice, a portrait of Rembrandt by one of his pupils, a Landseer and a library of some 3500 late 19th century books – are 4.8 hectares (12 acres) of gardens.

Somerleyton's yew hedge maze was designed by celebrated landscape gardener William Nesfield and is one of the finest in Britain.

A feature of particular interest in the stable block, next to the northern wing of the Hall, is the clock tower and timepiece – designed by Vulliamy, clock-maker to George II and IV, William IV and Victoria, and intended at one time for the Houses of Parliament.

Somerleyton is open to the public on Thursdays, Sundays and Bank Holidays from Easter through to the end of September, as well as on Tuesdays and Wednesdays in July and August.

Admission to the gardens is available between 12.30pm and 5.30pm and the Hall from 1pm to 5pm (last entry 4.30pm) with the Loggia tearoom serving light lunches and afternoon teas between 12.30pm and 5pm.

Suffolk Wildlife Park

This establishment at Kessingland, near Lowestoft, changed its name nine years ago, when it became the sister

Pleasurewood Hills
Tel. 01502 586000
e-mail: info@
pleasurewoodhills.co.uk
web: www.
pleasurewoodhills.co.uk

**Somerleyton Hall
(Administrator)**
Tel. 01502 730224
Fax. 01502 732143
e-mail: enquiries@
somerleyton.co.uk
web:
www.somerleyton.co.uk

Suffolk Wildlife Park
Tel. 01502 740291
Fax. 01502 741104
web: www.
suffolkwildlifepark.co.uk

attraction to Banham Zoo in Norfolk.

Set in 40 hectares (100 acres) of coastal parkland, it has an African theme and features lions, giraffes, hyenas, zebras and cheetahs among a variety of animals from that continent.

It is the only place in Britain where you can see aardvarks – unusual animals, threatened with extinction in the wild because of hunting and habitat destruction.

Visitors can walk any of three

Somerleyton Hall

Southwold promenade

explorer trails through woods, lakeland and grassy plains or enjoy a free ride aboard the Killimanjaro Safari Train with its commentary on fascinating animal facts.

For younger visitors there's a children's farmyard, adventure playground, bouncy castle and face painting.

Feeding time talks and animal-handling sessions for the public are daily from Easter to October.

Bird of prey displays, with hawks, falcons and other birds are three times daily on Mondays, Tuesdays, Wednesdays and Thursdays during the Summer holidays, when there is also various children's entertainment.

There is a free car and coach park with access, parking and wheelchairs available for disabled visitors.

Children must be accompanied by an adult at all times and no dogs or other pets allowed in park.

Opening times at the park are daily, except Christmas and Boxing Day, from 10am with closing at 5pm (until the end of June), 5.30pm (end of September), and 4pm (October to Easter). Last visitors one hour before closing.

Southwold

Amber Museum

Claimed to be the only museum in the world specifically dedicated to the history and story of amber.

Pieces on show at the purpose-built Southwold Market Place premises, which are open free of charge between 10am and 5pm from Monday to Saturday, include amber from all over the globe.

Lifeboat Museum

A small museum to be found at Gun Hill at the far end of Southwold.

Sailors' Reading Room

A quaint Southwold East Cliff building containing items of maritime interest.

Southwold Museum

A typical, Dutch-gabled cottage, containing many exhibits of local interest – including items from the old narrow gauge Southwold Railway.

Summer Theatre

Small repertory theatre at St Edmund's Hall, Cumberland Road, Southwold, where **Jill Freud and Company** presents a varied programme of plays and musicals.

Traditional Sailing Charter

A company which offers a range of trips – from four hours to full day – for individuals or groups of up to ten aboard the 1912 lugger Girl Sybil.

Skipper Marcus Gladwell and his wife Vicky, who own the vessel, have completed two round the world voyages.

The fully restored Girl Sybil, built to fish with drift nets, is based at Blackshore, Southwold Harbour – on the north bank of the River Blyth.

Southwold Area

Carriage Rides, Tannington Hall

Visitors to the village of Laxfield, near Halesworth, can enjoy leisurely carriage rides through the peaceful country lanes around nearby Tannington Hall.

A range of all-weather drives is available in genuine gypsy horse-drawn caravans between April and October, with a stop at the King's Head, Laxfield for drinks or lunch.

After a ride of two or two and a half hours, the six to eight passengers aboard return to the hall, where they can have lunch or a candle-lit evening meal or enjoy the gardens and stables and a collection of some

50 horse-drawn vehicles.

Tannington Hall is open from 9am to 7.30pm.

Dunwich Heath

Dunwich is an important, but rapidly-eroding, coastal reserve just to the North of Orford Ness.

The heath at Dunwich is spectacular in Summer and purple heather provides an excellent home for ground nesting birds like the stonechat and secretive nightjar.

Thanks to conservation efforts, the Dartford Warbler returned to the heath five years ago after an absence of six decades.

Dunwich, with its beach and good footpath network, is the National Trust's most popular East Anglian coastal property.

There is a first floor lookout point, with telescope, at Coastguard Cottages, which provide the focus for visitors to the heath, as well as a licensed restaurant, educational office and field study centre.

Guided walks with a warden are available throughout year and specially organised on request for groups (who must book in advance).

A Braille guide is available for visually-impaired visitors wishing to explore the site.

Dunwich Museum

A small but fascinating museum featuring local natural history and detailing the fate of the town from Roman times until most of it disappeared into the sea because of coastal erosion.

The museum is open between 2pm and 4.30pm on Saturdays and Sundays in March, between 11.30am and 4.30pm daily from the beginning of April to the end of September and between 12 noon and 4pm in October.

Laxfield and District Museum

Display of agricultural, geological, natural history and sartorial items in the 16th century Guildhall of this village south west of Halesworth.

The museum is open to the public between 2pm and 5pm on Saturdays, Sundays and Bank Holidays from May to September as well as between 2pm and 4pm on Wednesdays by arrangement.

Minsmere Nature Reserve

Minsmere, on the Suffolk coast at Westleton, is one of the RSPB's premier nature reserves, offering an enjoyable day out to both families and birdwatchers alike.

Nature trails take visitors through a variety of habitats to the excellent birdwatching hides and there is a programme of events throughout the year – including educational specials and attractions for those new to birdwatching.

In the Summer, avocets – for which Minsmere is the main British breeding area – as well as marsh harriers and ringed plovers can be seen and booming bitterns can be heard.

There are little terns, too – although a special area of beach is cordoned off to protect them at nesting time.

In the Autumn and Winter many wading birds and waterfowl visit the reserve.

Minsmere is also home to wild otters, which were successfully reintroduced to the reserve after being bred at Earsham, the Suffolk headquarters of the Otter Trust.

Facilities at Minsmere include a visitor centre, shop, tea-room, two nature trails and eight bird-watching hides with binocular hire and programmes for schools.

The visitor centre is open between 9am and 5pm from February to the end of October and between 9am and 4pm for the remaining three months of the year (closed Christmas Day, Boxing Day and Tuesdays).

The reserve is open between 9am and dusk (or 9pm if earlier) daily except for Tuesdays, Christmas Day and Boxing Day.

Dunwich Heath (NT)
Tel. 01728 648501

Dunwich Museum
Tel. 01728 648796

Laxfield and District Museum
Tel. 01986 798460 or 798421

Minsmere Nature Reserve
Tel. 01728 648281

Dunwich Heath

West Suffolk

An area boasting everything from the colour and excitement of action at racing's Newmarket Headquarters to the calm of historic Lavenham and the other famous wool villages.

It also boasts the ancient capital of East Anglia – where a King of the Angles and the sister of Henry VIII were buried.

Elsewhere in the area there are other attractions as diverse as a recreated Anglo-Saxon village and the beautiful but extraordinary Ickworth National Trust property at Horringer.

Kentwell Hall, Long Melford

Tourist Information Centres

Bury St Edmunds
Tel. 01284 764667; Fax. 01284 757084
e-mail: tic@stedsbc.gov.uk

East Bergholt (Open Easter to October)
Tel. 01206 299460
e-mail: tourism@babergh-south-suffolk.gov.uk

Lavenham (Open Easter to October and 11am–4pm in November)
Tel. 01787 248207
e-mail: tourism@babergh-south-suffolk.gov.uk

Newmarket
Tel. 01638 667200; Fax. 01638 660394
e-mail: palace-house-tic@fhdc.demon.co.uk

Stowmarket
Tel. 01449 676800; Fax. 01449 614691
e-mail: info@tic.keme.co.uk

Sudbury
Tel. 01787 881320
e-mail: tourism@babergh-south-suffolk.gov.uk

Ordnance Survey Maps
OS Landranger sheet numbers: 154, 155

The Theatre Royal, Bury St Edmunds

Bury St Edmunds

Bury St Edmunds, the ancient capital of East Anglia, features the intriguing remains of a great and historic Abbey and a medieval street plan containing Georgian houses and quaint shops.

Dickens stayed at the ancient **Angel Hotel,** on nearby Angel Hill, and today's guests can step back into the past by dining in the brasserie-styled 12th century vaults.

Abbey

Stone ruins mark the site of one of the wealthiest and most powerful abbeys in the whole of England and the burial place of a King of the East Angles martyred by the Danes.

Perhaps the most surprising person to discover buried in the town is Mary Tudor, sister to Henry VIII.

Some 4000 people walked from Westhorpe to Bury Abbey for her funeral, which lasted a day and a half in 1533.

Six years later, when Henry dissolved the monasteries, Mary's body was moved to St Mary's Church in Bury.

The Abbey visitor centre is open from Easter to the end of October.

Greene King Brewery

The company, which has been brewing in Bury for more than 200 years, now has an interactive visitor centre on site and offers a 'Brewery Tour Experience' at any time of year.

Manor House Museum

The museum, in a restored 18th century Georgian mansion, houses collections of costumes, fine and decorative arts and rare clocks and watches with other constantly-changing exhibitions, lectures and workshops.

The Manor House is open between 12 noon and 5pm from Sunday to Wednesday.

Moyse's Hall Museum

A 12th century Norman town house containing not only a lock of Mary Tudor's hair but also grisly relics of the notorious 'Red Barn Murder', mummified cats and the largest Bronze Age hoard found in Western Europe.

The museum – in previous times variously a gaol, police station, railway parcels office and tavern – is normally open between 10am and 5pm from Monday to Saturday and 2pm and 5pm on Sundays all year round.

But, **please note**, it will be closed for a major refurbishment project from September 2000 to September 2001.

St Edmundsbury Cathedral

The 16th century nave of St James, with its fine hammer beam roof,

Angel Hotel
Tel. 01284 753926
Fax. 01284 750092
web: www.theangel.co.uk

Abbey Visitor Centre
Tel. 01284 763110

Greene King Brewery
tour office
Tel. 01284 714382
museum
Tel. 01284 714297
Fax. 01284 714538
web: www.greeneking.co.uk

Manor House Museum
Tel. 01284 757076 or 757072
Fax. 01284 757079
web:
www.stedmundsbury.gov.uk/
manorhse.htm

Moyse's Hall Museum
Tel. 01284 757488
Fax. 01284 757489
web:
www.stedmundsbury.gov.uk/
moyses.htm

St Edmundsbury Cathedral
Tel. 01284 754933
shop
Tel. 01284 764205
Fax. 01284 768655
web:
www.stedscathedral.co.uk

Theatre Royal
box office
Tel. 01284 769505
admin
Tel. 01284 755127
Fax. 01284 706035
web: www.theatreroyal.org

became the Cathedral of Suffolk in 1914, since when it has been considerably extended.

Theatre Royal

One of the jewels of modern Bury is its beautifully-restored late Georgian playhouse, which opened in 1819 and is now administered by the National Trust.

The theatre, in Westgate Street, is open between 10.15am and 8pm daily for visits (except Sundays and Bank Holidays and when in use for performances).

The Nutshell

Located in The Traverse, this Greene King pub claims to be the smallest in Britain.

Bury St Edmunds Area

Burwell Museum and Steven's Mill

This attraction includes a 17th century timber barn, smithy and wheelwright's shop, granary and wagon sheds.

There is a telephone exchange visitors can try out and exhibits feature wartime Burwell, early agriculture and local industries.

The site is open between 2pm and 5pm on Sundays, Thursdays and Bank Holiday Mondays from Easter until the end of September.

Gifford's Hall Vineyard and Sweet Pea Centre

Gifford's Hall is set in 13.5 hectares (33 acres) of countryside at Hartest, near Bury St Edmunds.

Today nearly 12,000 grapevines form the backbone of the business, whose attractions include vineyards and a winery, producing some fine English wines, as well as sweet pea, rose and mainly organic vegetable gardens.

Visitors can see for themselves how the vines are grown and can then taste the wines and learn how they are made.

Gifford's Hall also produces a variety of home-made liqueurs using old-fashioned country recipes. Visitors over the age of 18 are offered a free tasting.

The Hall is set in some of Suffolk's loveliest farmland and there are 2.4 kilometres (1½ miles) of country walks along wide grass paths to enjoy.

Refreshments are served in the tearoom and the farm shop sells all surplus produce, including free-range eggs, organic vegetables and honey.

Gifford's Hall, where there are also children's play and picnic areas, is open daily between 11am and 6pm from Easter to the end of October.

Henry Watson's Potteries

These Wattisfield-based potteries, near Bury, produce the popular brown terracotta 'Original Suffolk' kitchenware range.

The site includes a coffee shop and a factory shop selling good quality seconds.

Ickworth House

This former home of the Marquis of Bristol is now opened to the public by the National Trust.

The present Ickworth House, at Horringer, south west of Bury, was only built at the turn of the 19th century – having been conceived by Frederick, the Fourth Earl of Bristol, who landed the unlikely job of Bishop of Derry in Ireland.

He developed a taste for round buildings during his European travels and Ickworth was designed first and foremost to house his rapidly expanding collection. But many of his treasures never made it back home.

Today Ickworth still contains Regency and 18th century pictures and furniture as well as Georgian silver.

The National Trust shop on site sells, among other things, wine from the Shawsgate Vineyard – which is based in the old, brick-walled kitchen gardens.

The house is open to the public daily (except Mondays – other than Bank Holidays – and Thursdays) between 1pm and 5pm (4pm in October) from mid-March to the end

Nutshell public house
Tel. 01284 764867
web: www.greeneking.co.uk

Burwell Museum and Steven's Mill
Tel. 01638 741713

Gifford's Hall Vineyard
Tel. 01284 830464
Fax. 01284 830964
web: www.giffordshall.co.uk

Henry Watson's Potteries
Tel. 01359 251239
Fax. 01359 250984
web:
www.henrywatson.com

Ickworth House (N.T.)
Tel. 01284 735270
Fax. 01284 735270
web:
www.nationaltrust.org.uk

Gifford's Hall sweet pea centre

of October.

The Italian gardens are open daily between 10am and 5pm over the same period as well as between 10am and 4pm Monday to Friday in November and from the beginning of January to the middle of March.

Ickworth's park and deer enclosure is open daily throughout the year.

Newmarket

The **horse racing** industry has had a considerable impact on the town, which is surrounded by chalk heathland where Medieval horsemen practised their riding skills.

But it was James I, in 1605, who began Newmarket's transformation – continued for the remainder of the Stuart period – into the unofficial second capital of England.

Horse racing was firmly established at this time and the sport has enjoyed royal patronage at Newmarket ever since, with the racing season now running from April to October.

The National Horseracing Museum, next to the imposing High Street headquarters of The Jockey Club, offers visitors the chance to try on racing silks and climb into the saddle on a mechanical horse.

It is open between 10am and 5pm from Tuesday to Saturday from Easter to the end of October and also between the same times on Mondays in July and August.

A daily **Newmarket Tour** takes in the gallops, the horses' swimming pool and a training yard as well as a guide to the town.

The tour which lasts around two hours, departs at 9.20am on every museum opening day and includes admission to the museum. Advance booking is advisable due to limited places on the tour.

Other available tours include 'An Introduction to Racing', 'Private Stud Tour' and 'Dick Francis Tour'.

Daily visits to the **National Stud** – opened by the Queen in 1967 and one of the most prestigious in the country – last around 75 minutes and are available from March to September and on race days in October.

Occasionally included as part of one of the Museum's programmes,

Ickworth House, Horringer

the tours take in the stallion unit, stallions in residence and nursery yards as well as mares and foals in their paddocks.

Tours depart at 11.15am and 2.30pm Monday to Saturday (2.30pm tour only on Sunday).

Members of the public can also visit the world-famous **Tattersalls,** at Terrace House & Paddocks, Newmarket, and watch the sale of thoroughbred horses fetching many thousands of pounds.

The **Animal Health Trust,** based at Lanwades Hall on the outskirts of Newmarket, is the only charitable institution in the country engaged in the full-time diagnosis, cure and prevention of animal diseases.

It includes a visitor centre – open between 10am and 4pm from Monday to Friday – which was opened by the Princess Royal in 1998 and features exhibitions and touch screens.

Tours of the complex itself are available but must be pre-booked.

Nowton Park

The park, just off the A134, southeast of Bury St Edmunds, consists of nearly 81 hectares (200 acres) of beautiful Suffolk countryside, an area landscaped more than a hundred years ago in typical Victorian style.

Until 1985, the park formed part of the Oakes Family estate. But it is now owned and managed by the St.

Newmarket Racecourses Trust
Tel. 01638 663482
Fax. 01638 663044
web: www.newmarket racecourses.co.uk

National Horseracing Museum
Tel. 01638 667333
Fax. 01638 665600
web: www.nhrm.co.uk

Hooffbeats Newmarket Guided Tours
Tel./Fax. 01638 578628
e-mail:
hoofbeats@cwcom.net
web: www.hoofbeats.co.uk

National Stud
office
Tel. 01638 663464
tour line
Tel. 01638 666789
Fax. 01638 665173
web:
www.nationalstud.co.uk

Tattersalls
Tel. 01638 665931
Fax. 01638 660850

Animal Health Trust
Tel. 01638 751000
Fax. 01638 750410
www.aht.org.uk

Nowton Park
Tel. 01284 763666

Joanna Pinnock and Paul Heiney at Rede Hall Farm

West Stow Anglo-Saxon Village

Reconstruction of an Anglo-Saxon village at Icklingham Road, West Stow (just north of Bury St Edmunds), based on ancient foundations discovered at the site.

It is open daily between 10am and 5pm and there are special events throughout the year as well as guided tours and walks.

Stowmarket

A small but busy market town in the heart of rural Suffolk, Stowmarket was once involved in the wool trade, which was conducted with Ipswich via the River Gipping.

The Museum of East Anglian Life

Set in the heart of Stowmarket, the museum includes various collections connected with East Anglia's rural past on an attractive 28-hectare (70-acre) riverside site.

There are displays on gypsy caravans and domestic and agricultural life as well as carts and wagons, a chapel, craft shops, farm implements, an industrial workshop and smithy, steam engines and a working watermill and wind pump.

All of the buildings of historic interest, apart from Abbot's Hall Barn, have been moved specially to the site from elsewhere in the region.

The museum, which also features an adventure playground, café, gift shop and picnic area, is open between 10am and 5pm from Monday to Saturday and 11am and 5pm on Sundays from April to October.

Stowmarket Area

Baylham House

A rare breeds farm on the site of a Roman settlement at Mill Lane, Baylham, featuring cattle, sheep, poultry, goats and pigs.

Among breeds of sheep on the farm are Greyface Dartmoors, Castlemilk Moorits (the rarest British species, with fewer than 300 registered females), Llanwenogs, Norfolk Horns, Balwen and Herdwick.

There are paddocks where the animals can be fed as well as a picnic area, riverside walk and visitor centre with shop and refreshments.

Baylham House, between Great Blakenham and Needham Market, is open at 11am daily from Tuesday to Sunday as well as on Bank Holiday Mondays from the end of March to the beginning of October and over the October half-term holiday.

Bradfield Woods Nature Reserve

Possibly the best surviving example of ancient woodland in Britain, Bradfield, west of Stowmarket, is home to the common dormouse among other animals.

Bradfield has both a car park and visitor centre.

Mechanical Music & Bygones Museum

A veritable Aladdin's cave of musical treasures at Cotton, near Stowmarket – with roof rafters decorated with numerous old gramophone records and horn gramophones.

The rafters are almost reached

Edmundsbury Borough Council for recreation, leisure and nature conservation.

Pakenham Water Mill

A Grade II listed working mill, complete with oil engine and other machinery, on its original Domesday site.

Rede Hall Farm Park

This working farm, on the A143 between Bury and Haverhill, is based on agricultural life between the 1930s and 1950s.

There are rare breeds of farm animals as well as working Suffolk and Shire horses with cart and pony rides included in the admission price.

Rede Hall, which has a children's pet area, gift shop, small museum and tearoom on site, is open between 10am and 5pm daily from the beginning of April to the end of September.

from below by fairground organs from famous makers and there are barrel, player and reed models as well as a gigantic café organ and a Wurlitzer which started life in Brooklyn and arrived via London's Leicester Square Theatre.

Pianolas also feature in the museum along with musical boxes, a musical Christmas tree and musical chair, organettes and polyphons.

The museum is open, with conducted tours, between 2.30pm and 5.30pm on Sundays from June to September.

Mid-Suffolk Light Railway Museum

Suffolk's only railway museum was created by a group of enthusiasts on the site of Brockford Station at Wetheringsett, north-east of Stowmarket, nearly 40 years after the Mid-Suffolk line closed in 1952.

It contains original buildings, a Hudson Clarke steam locomotive and Great Eastern coaches – one of them offering refreshments as well as books and souvenirs and a display of photographs and memorabilia.

Needham Lake

This area, east of Stowmarket, was created in the early 1970's when sand and gravel was extracted from the site to build the nearby A14 trunk road.

In 1980 the 11-hectare (27-acre) council-owned site was developed to support a wide variety of wildlife through a large wildflower meadow and a small woodland area called Kings Meadow, which has been designated as a local nature reserve.

Over the years the council's countryside team has managed the site to encourage wildlife. Trees have been planted and the long grass is only cut once a year, enabling more grasses and wild flowers to grow.

Species are increasing all the time, with a population of orchids and the scarce wild liquorice plant taking root.

For more information contact Countryside Officer Richard Thurlow at Mid Suffolk District Council.

Sudbury

Another small but attractive rural Suffolk market town – known best perhaps for Gainsborough, who lived in the town in the 18th century and produced many paintings of the surrounding area.

Sudbury Area

Carlton Llama Farm

Maggie and Michael Warner were so enchanted by llamas during a visit to South America that they decided to set up their own breeding herd at their Thorpe Morieux farm.

They now have about 40 animals and specialise in breeding coloured varieties for natural fibres, which can be spun, woven and knitted into a variety of appealing garments.

Related to camels, llamas are highly intelligent and graceful creatures which migrated about three million years ago to South America, where they are among the world's oldest domesticated animals.

They are still used by the native population in the Andes for transport, meat, wool-like coats and milk.

Thorpe Morieux is at the centre of a square between the towns of Bury St Edmunds, Stowmarket, Sudbury and Hadleigh and is about 16 kilometres (ten miles) from each.

The farm is in Thorpe Green Lane, opposite the church and 50 metres (55 yards) from the main village sign on the green.

Pre-booked special interest groups are welcome, by appointment. But, regrettably, neither children under 6 nor dogs are admitted.

There is no admission charge but visitors are asked to make a donation to Cancer Research, which has already received several thousand pounds.

Cavendish

The picture postcard village of Cavendish with its thatched houses and 14th/15th century church is also the home of the **Sue Ryder Foundation Museum,** which contains war memorabilia and photographs and tells the story of the institution's

Mid-Suffolk Light
Railway Museum
Tel. 01449 766899

Carlton Llama Farm
Tel. 01284 828227
Fax. 01284 828985
e-mail: mwarner@
acs.pennylane.com

Sue Ryder Foundation
Museum
Tel. 01787 282591
Fax. 01787 280548

Cavendish

beginnings and its work up to the present.

The museum, which serves lunches and refreshments, is open daily between 10am and 5.30pm throughout the year.

Clare

The picturesque and historic village of Clare, which was one of only six boroughs in Suffolk at the time of the Norman Conquest, contains the ruins of a 13ᵗʰ century monastery and monastic church.

Clare Castle Country Park
Tel. 01787 277491

Clare Ancient House Museum
Tel. 01787 277520
web:
www.stedmundsbury.gov.uk/
wtsee.htm or
www.cvr.org.uk

Gainsborough's House
Tel. 01787 372958
Fax. 01787 376991
web: www.gainsborough.org

Hadleigh Guildhall
Tel. 01473 823884
web: www.hadleigh.org.uk/
or www.hadleigh-
suffolk.co.uk

Kentwell Hall
Tel. 01787 310207
Fax. 01787 379318
web: www.kentwell.co.uk

Clare

It also boasts the remains of a Norman castle, which are set in Suffolk's oldest public **country park** with its 10 hectares (25 acres) of riverside and woodland walks and visitor centre housed in Clare's former railway station.

The village itself boasts a rich architectural heritage which includes timbered and pargetted facades along the streets and a **museum** – which is open every afternoon from Thursday to Sunday as well as between at least 2pm and 5pm on Bank Holiday Mondays from May to September.

Gainsborough's House

A Georgian-fronted, walled-gardened house which was the birthplace of the celebrated artist Thomas Gainsborough (1727–1788).

It has now been turned into a treasure house of his work, holding more examples than any other British gallery.

The museum is open between 10am and 5pm from Tuesday to Saturday and 2pm and 5pm (4pm closing in Winter) on Sundays and Bank Holiday Mondays throughout the year (except from Christmas to New Year).

Hadleigh

A village known for its history and offering every kind of domestic Suffolk architecture for inspection along the High Street.

As with Lavenham, Hadleigh rose to prosperity on the back of the wool trade and perhaps its grandest buildings are the timber-framed buildings of the 15ᵗʰ/16ᵗʰ century Guildhall, church and Deanery Tower.

The Guildhall, originally a market house, guildhall and wool hall, is open be-

Lavenham Guildhall

tween 2pm and 5pm on Thursdays and Sundays from June to September.

The great outdoors is not far away – with many nature reserves within walking distance of the High Street – and country walks and cycle paths surround the village.

Kentwell Hall

Kentwell Hall at Long Melford, on the Suffolk/Essex border, is a red brick Tudor Mansion surrounded by a broad moat.

It has been described as "the epitome of many people's image of an Elizabethan house" and a visit, particularly for the special re-creation events, is like stepping back in time.

Attractions include the house, moat house, gardens, farm and yeoman's cottage, all set up to reflect 16ᵗʰ century life, as well as more up-to-date facilities like refreshments, gift shop and toilets with access for people with disabilities.

To really capture the flavour of Tudor life, visit during one of the special events, particularly the Grand Re-creation, when house and grounds are filled with people authentically dressed to portray characters from the past – such as stewards and pages, cooks and dairymaids, archers and potters, ostlers and players.

Kentwell, which was used as the setting for Toad Hall in the Terry

Jones film Wind in the Willows, is on the Suffolk/Essex border, off the A134, between Bury St Edmunds and Sudbury.

It is open for various events at different times in various weeks from the middle of April to the beginning of September excluding most of May and the first two weeks of June (please phone for details).

Lavenham

Well known as one of Suffolk's prettiest villages, Lavenham is steeped in history – with perhaps more medieval timber houses per square foot than anywhere else in England.

The market place is dominated by the **Guildhall,** an early 16th century timber framed building now owned by the National Trust and open daily between 11am and 5pm from late April to the beginning of November.

Inside are exhibitions on local history, farming and industry, along with a display which focuses on the medieval wool trade.

The magnificent 'Wool Church' of St Peter & St Paul, meanwhile, has one of the tallest towers in East Anglia.

Melford Hall

A National Trust property featuring rooms of various styles in a turreted Tudor mansion and a collection of Chinese porcelain.

The gardens are open between 2pm and 5.30pm on Saturdays, Sundays and Bank Holidays in April, from Wednesday to Sunday as well as Bank Holidays between May and September and on Saturdays and Sundays in October.

The Hall, Milden

This hall, near Lavenham, is a listed, Georgianised, 16th century farmhouse surrounded by ancient wildflower meadows, barns and walled gardens.

There are planned farm nature trail routes for exploring the farm, meadows, award-winning woodland, ponds, and Norman castle earthworks.

Quay Theatre

Housed in a restored maltings on a cut from the River Stour at Sudbury, the theatre offers a wide range of entertainment, including films and plays, throughout the year.

River Trips from Sudbury

The **Rosette,** an electric launch owned by the River Stour Trust, operates river trips to Cornard Lock from The Granary in Quay Lane on Sundays and Bank Holidays between 11.30am and 5.15pm from Easter to October.

Lavenham Guildhall
Tel. 01787 247646
web: www.lavenham.co.uk/
or www.touruk.co.uk

Melford Hall (N.T.)
Tel. 01787 880286
web:
www.nationaltrust.org.uk

The Hall, Milden
Tel./Fax. 01787 247235
e-mail: gjb53@dial.pipex.com

**Quay Theatre
(box office)**
Tel. 01787 374745
Fax. 01787 312602
e-mail: mmunn@
thequay37.fsnet.co.uk

M/V Rosette
Tel. 01787 211507 or 372602

**Lavenham Rare Breeds
Motor Show**
Tel. 01787 247893
e-mail:
bryan.panton@virgin.net

Vintage Cars

Lavenham's Rare Breeds Motor Show was established in 1995 and is normally held as part of Lavenham Carnival week-end in August.

Showing a car at the festival is free and entries are welcome from both previous and new exhibitors.

Melford Hall

East Suffolk

 Last Suffolk has a long and often beautiful coastline with something for almost everyone and considerable stretches of Heritage Coast, set in an Area of Outstanding Natural Beauty.

Huge skies cover expanses of beautiful countryside, taking in poppy fields, ancient woods, nature reserves and country parks.

It's a good area for walking and riding with plenty of footpaths for both long and short distance excursions as well as a large number of bridleways.

From Aldeburgh to Felixstowe there are Martello Towers, built to guard against the threat of Napoleonic invasion – but these days the only intruders are friendly and are made more than welcome.

i Tourist Information Centres

Aldeburgh (Easter to October)
Tel./Fax. 01728 453637

Felixstowe
Tel. 01394 276770; Fax. 01394 277456

Ipswich
Tel. 01473 258070; Fax. 01473 432017
e-mail: tourist@ipswich.gov.uk

Mid Suffolk (Stowmarket)
Tel. 01449 676800; Fax. 01449 614691
e-mail: info@tic.keme.co.uk

Woodbridge
Tel. 01394 382240; Fax. 01394 386337
e-mail: wtic@suffolkcoastal.gov.uk

Ordnance Survey Maps

OS Landranger sheet number: 156

Post mill and The House in the Clouds, Thorpeness

Aldeburgh

Originally a fishing port and small market town, Aldeburgh has made its name throughout the world because of its associations with the arts – including literature and, especially, music.

The town has been cast as the setting or starting point for many books, including The Woman in White by Wilkie Collins.

On the musical front, pride of place goes to Lowestoft-born **Benjamin Britten** who, along with **Peter Pears,** founded the Aldeburgh Festival in 1947.

The town's entertainment programme includes a season of Summer repertory theatre with **Jill Freud and Company** – who also perform at Southwold – at The Jubilee Hall, just off the High Street.

One of Aldeburgh's most famous buildings is its old meeting place, the medieval Moot Hall, which once marked the Tudor centre of town.

Now, because of coastal erosion over the centuries, it stands just back from the shingle beach, where fisherman still haul up their boats.

Aldeburgh Area

Sizewell Visitor Centre

A permanent exhibition about energy, the environment and nuclear power that is open to the public between Easter and October (phone for opening times).

Guided tours of the power stations at Sizewell are offered by prior arrangement.

Snape Maltings and Concert Hall

A riverside collection of 19th century buildings, just south of the small village of Snape, containing shops, galleries and restaurants open daily all year round between 10am and 6pm (5pm in Winter).

The splendid setting is also home to the world-famous concert hall, with its superb acoustics, which

Snape Maltings and Concert Hall

offers a year-round programme of music and dance.

The Aldeburgh Festival of Music and the Arts takes place here in June, while Snape Proms – which feature a series of world, classical, jazz and folk concerts – are held in August.

Thorpeness

A small village north of Aldeburgh which features a well-known local landmark called **The House in the Clouds.**

This remarkable structure was built in 1923 and was originally a steel-framed water tower with accommodation below.

The tank was removed in the 1970s and converted into further accommodation, which is hired out on a self-catering basis.

Thorpeness is also known for The Meare – a splendid boating lake inspired by Peter Pan author J.M. Barrie, with rowing boats and canoes available for hire each day from Easter to October.

Orford

Just south of Aldeburgh, Orford is steeped in history and was once a town and Royal stronghold with an important harbour.

But by Tudor times ocean-going ships could no longer enter the harbour because of the vagaries of the sea, which deposited shingle and gravel from further along the coast, and today the harbour is dry land.

The road to what is now a pleasant, peaceful village passes through the primeval forest of Staverton Park

– one of only two such forests in England – and herds of deer can often be seen in the early morning or early evening.

Orford's quay is the year-round embarkation point for lunch, brunch or dinner river cruises aboard the 35-ton ex-Admiralty vessel **Lady Florence,** while another vessel, **Regardless,** offers one-hour trips around Havergate Island from April to October.

Orford Castle

Orford Castle

Watching over the approaches to what was once a flourishing port are the remains of a mighty Norman fortress, which continues as a formidable landmark 800 years after it was built.

Although it's hard to believe, looking at the charming but isolated village today, Orford was considered a rival to Portsmouth as one of England's most important and powerful naval ports at the time of Henry II.

On his orders the marshes around Orford were drained in 1165 and within two years one of the most complex and expensive castles in England had been built.

Today the three-storey keep on a grassy mound – or motte, as it was then called – is all that is left of one of the oldest castles in England.

But most of the documentary evidence about it survives remarkably intact to reveal a detailed picture of what life there in the 12th century was really like.

The castle, which features parking and a shop on site, is open daily between 10am and 6pm in Summer (5pm in October) and between 10am and 4pm (closed 1–2pm) from Wednesday to Sunday in Winter.

Underwater Exploration Exhibition

An interesting permanent exhibition of marine archaeology and coastal erosion, including Dunwich Bank artefacts.

The exhibition, which is housed upstairs in The Craft Shop at Front Street, Orford, is open daily between 11am and 5pm all year round.

Orford Area

Havergate Island

This small island is in the River Ore, 32 kilometres (20 miles) from Ipswich, at the southern end of the most easterly stretch of coastline in the British Isles.

It is a prime example of one of more than a hundred reserves managed by the RSPB – a Grade 1 SSI site – consisting mainly of shallow lagoons containing small islands and mudflats for breeding birds and wintering waders.

Between 25 and 30 species of birds breed at Havergate and around 150 different species are recorded there in any one year – including short-eared and barn owls and at least one hen harrier.

No fewer than 134 species were identified in the annual plant survey, including Sea Parslane, which covers the island's saltmarsh at times, and the white-flowered Scurvy Grass.

Havergate also has an active population of small animals including a colony of more than 50 hares, which are easily seen at the southern end of the island and from the hides.

For butterfly fans there is the chance to see some of the 17 species recorded on the island. Among the commonest are the Essex and Small Skippers and Meadow and Wall Browns.

Havergate is accessible by boat from Orford – but only if permits are booked in advance, as the boat carries a maximum of ten passengers at any one time.

The island can be visited between 10am and approximately 3.30pm on the first and third Saturdays and Sundays of the month as well as every Thursday from April until August, while from September until March visiting is on the first Saturday of the month only.

Visitors should assemble in good time (according to booking) for the trip across to the island as the boat will not wait.

Cars must not be parked at Orford quay – there is plenty of parking in the new car park at the back of the quay.

Written applications for permits to visit the island – no telephone calls will be accepted – must be sent in advance to The Warden at 30 Mundays Lane, Orford, Woodbridge, Suffolk IP12 2LX.

There is a special picnic area near the reception point on the island, with toilets nearby, and eight hides can be found along the eastern, seaward shore of the island.

A booklet on the reserve is available from the Woodbridge group of the RSPB at 42a Bredfield Road, Woodbridge, Suffolk.

Orford Ness

Also accessible via a short boat trip from Orford, the Ness was forbidden territory from 1915 until the 1970s – bearing notices warning that it was Government Property and only authorised persons were allowed to land.

In fact it was an important

A Martello tower on the coast near Orford

military research site and was used by Robert Watson-Watt to carry out early experiments with radar in 1935 and later by Barnes Wallis and other pioneers working on bomb ballistics and firing trials.

Surviving buildings include huge concrete 'pagodas' constructed by the Atomic Weapons Research Establishment in the 1960s.

The National Trust bought eight kilometres (five miles) of the Ness – comprising 607 hectares (1500 acres) of shingle and saltmarsh – from the Ministry of Defence for £3½ million in April 1993.

Just over two years later, in June 1995, members of the public were allowed on to the Ness for the first time since the First World War.

Orford Ness is remarkable as one of the very few remaining wild areas of coast in Southern England and is the most important vegetated spit in the United Kingdom.

The five-minute ferry crossing from Orford also takes visitors to what is now an internationally-known breeding colony for lesser black-backed gulls.

Contact the warden, Grant Lahoar for details of guided walks – which are available from May to October – as well as information on educational visits and resources.

For up to date details of ferry crossing and availability (advance booking is essential) contact the Orford Ness ferry information line.

Ipswich

Ipswich has a large shopping centre, numerous theatres and cinemas, beautiful parks, four sports centres, indoor and outdoor swimming pools and a varied collection of pubs, clubs and other night life.

The county town of Suffolk also boasts a history dating from Saxon times and numerous fascinating buildings, galleries and museums.

The latter include **Christchurch Mansion,** a fine Tudor house set in beautiful Christchurch park, with period rooms displayed in styles ranging from the 16th to the 19th century.

There are impressive collections of furniture, china, clocks and glass as well as paintings by Suffolk artists including Constable and Gainsborough.

Ipswich Museum in the High Street, brings Anglo-Saxon times to life and there are displays of rocks, fossils and minerals together with one of the country's best collections of British birds.

The Ancient House, with its elaborate pargetting, is just one of many timber-framed buildings in Ipswich and 12 medieval churches are testimony to the importance of the town in the Middle Ages.

Ipswich Transport Museum at the Old Trolleybus Depot in Cobham Road and **Peter's Ice Cream Factory** in Grimwade Street (tours at 10am, midday, 2pm and 4pm – but by appointment only) are two other diverse attractions.

The family of poet Geoffrey Chaucer owned a tavern in Ipswich and, more recently, the late cartoonist Giles lived nearby. A statue of his 'Grandma' stands in Princes Street.

The Tolly Cobbold Brewery, first built in the 18th century and rebuilt 100 years ago, is one of the finest Victorian breweries in the country and is open for guided tours.

**Orford Castle
(English Heritage)**
Tel. 01394 450472

**Underwater Exploration
Exhibition**
Tel. 01394 450678

Havergate Island (Warden)
Tel/Fax. 01394 450732

**Orford Ness
(Ferry information line)**
Tel. 01394 450057

Orford Ness (NT Warden)
Tel./Fax. 01394 450900

Christchurch Mansion
Tel. 01473 433554 or 433563
Fax. 01473 433564

Ipwich Museum
Tel. 01473 433550
Fax. 01473 433558

Ipswich Transport Museum
Tel. 01473 715666

Peter's Ice Cream
Tel. 01473 253265

Tolly Cobbold Brewery
Tel. 01473 231723
Fax. 01473 280045
e-mail: tolly. cobbold@
btconnect.com
web:
www.tollycobbold.co.uk

Orford village and the Ness

Helmingham Hall
Tel. 01473 890363
Fax. 01473 890776
e-mail: helminghamestate@
aol.com

Stonham Barns
Tel./Fax. 01449 711755

**Birds of Prey &
Conservation Centre**
Tel./Fax. 01449 711425
e-mail:
owl.barn@btinternet.com
web:
www.the-owl-barn.com

**Suffolk Waters
Country Park**
Tel. 01473 830191

**Woolverstone
Barge Cruises**
Tel. 01473 780886

Ipswich Area

Helmingham Hall

Helmingham, down a long drive near Stowmarket, 14 kilometres (nine miles) north of Ipswich in Suffolk, is one of the East of England's most magnificent country houses.

Unfortunately the house, a gem of Elizabethan architecture, is not open to the public. But the gardens, equally famous in their own right, have become one of the most sought-after visitor attractions in the area.

Beyond the gardens lie 162 hectares (400 acres) of glorious rolling parkland through which visitors can take safari rides to see herds of 500 red and fallow deer whose ancestors were introduced around 1660 – as well as Highland cattle and Soay sheep.

One tradition remains intact from the day the building was completed. Every evening, when the visitors have gone, the working drawbridge is raised and Helmingham becomes once more a private fortress home.

The gardens at Helmingham are open to the public between 2pm and 6pm on Sunday afternoons from the beginning of May to early September

Birds of Prey & Conservation Centre, Stonham Barns

and also, by appointment only, to organised groups between 2pm and 5pm on Wednesday afternoons.

Cream teas are served in the old Coach House and there are also farm and gift shops.

Stonham Barns

Home of the **British Birds of Prey & Conservation Centre** – one of the premier raptor centres in the UK – where more than 60 owls and birds of prey can be seen in aviaries or flying free.

The complex includes an information centre, falconry centre, hospital and Owl Barn gift shop and there are picnic areas and plenty of activities for children.

The neighbouring Nature Centre offers an opportunity to meet a variety of domestic and other animals, including red squirrels.

It also features a butterfly meadow, childrens' activities, conservation projects, a nature trail and pond dipping.

As well as the two main bird and animal centres, Stonham's facilities also include 20 craft and gift shops, a coffee shop, garden centre and restaurant plus a driving range and nine-hole golf course.

Both the Birds of Prey

Centre and Nature Centre are open between 10.30am and late afternoon seven days a week and flying displays are staged three times daily from March to October.

Suffolk Waters Country Park

Based on a beautifully situated lake at Bramford, near Ipswich, this country park offers opportunities for canoeing, caravanning, cycling, fishing, rowing, walking and, as a RYA recognised centre, windsurfing.

Bicycles, canoes, rowing boats and sailboards can all be hired and instruction is available, if required, for both would-be canoeists and windsurfers.

A variety of hot and cold snacks are available at the park's own cafeteria.

Woolverstone Marina

The barge Thistle operates cruises for up to 50 people along the River Orwell daily from 9.30am between March and September.

Parties of 12 people or fewer can travel on smaller barges.

Woodbridge

This attractive small riverside town has a strong sailing 'feel' about it – and boasts a busy quayside and marina.

Two of the main structural features of Woodbridge are the Tide Mill – thought to be one of the earliest of its type in England – and the ancient Shire Hall.

Woolverstone Marina

The more modern **Riverside complex** contains a 265-seater cinema/ theatre as well as a garden-style restaurant and bar.

Shire Hall

This handsome structure, built by Elizabethan courtier Thomas Seckford, originally housed the Sessions – and iron doors to two cells can be seen at the eastern end.

After a pre-war spell as a corn market, the building was returned to court use – until bought by the Town Council in 1987.

The Council Chamber and administrative offices occupy the ground floor while the first floor is home to the Suffolk Horse Museum (q.v.).

Suffolk Horse Museum

The museum, on the first floor of the Market Hill Shire Hall, features the history of the breed and its Society, the world of shows and showing, the work of the horses and the life of the horseman.

A collection of paintings, historic photographs and silver complements displays in settings including a 1930s office, a blacksmith's shop, a horseman's kitchen and a harness-maker's workshop.

This unique and award-winning museum provides for a wide variety of interests and age groups and is open daily between 2pm and 5pm from Easter Monday to the end of September.

Tide Mill

This striking 18th century timber building occupies a waterfront site where earlier versions stood as far back as the 12th century and, in the Middle Ages, Augustinian monks operated the machinery.

It is open to the public between 11am and 5pm at Easter, on weekends in April and October and daily from early May to early September.

WI Country Markets

The WI co-operative markets were originally set up in 1917 to help the war effort – and there are now 517 of them throughout the country.

These popular markets generally sell good quality, home-grown and home-made produce from the garden and kitchen, as well as craftwork.

The Woodbridge market was set up in 1989/90 and is the largest market in East Suffolk.

It is held on Thursdays from 10am–11.15am at Woodbridge Community Centre – with tables set up at 8am and produce for sale booked in at 9am – and is regularly attended by some 200 people.

Despite the name, WI markets are not actually part of the Women's Institute, which is a separate organisation.

Woodbridge Museum

Contains displays focusing on the history of the town and its residents, including Edward Fitzgerald and Thomas Seckford, as well as a permanent exhibition on the nearby Sutton Hoo Anglo-Saxon site (q.v.).

The museum is open between 10am and 4pm from Thursday to Saturday and 2.30pm and 4.30pm on Sundays from Easter to the end of October as well as daily (except Wednesdays) in school Summer holidays.

Woodbridge Area

Akenfield Garden

One property stands out from the rest in a row of ordinary semi-detached houses on the eastern edge of the village of Charsfield, west of Wickham Market.

It's the house – with what started out as a small patch of overgrown land – to which Peggy Cole moved with her husband, Ernie, in the late 1950s.

But, since then, there's been a miraculous transformation – with half the plot given over to vegetables and every inch of what was left filled with more colour and diversity than can be found in gardens many times

the size.

Peggy's garden at 1 Park Lane, Charsfield, is open to the public – but BY APPOINTMENT ONLY!

Easton Farm Park

Easton, set in 14 hectares (35 acres) of countryside, first opened 25 years ago and is home to a large number of different animals ranging from rabbits to Suffolk Punch Horses.

All the animals are very friendly and can be stroked and fed by

Easton Farm Park

Riverside Complex
box office
Tel. 01394 382174
restaurant
Tel. 01394 382587
web:
www.theriverside.co.uk

Suffolk Horse Museum
Tel. 01394 380643

Tide Mill
Tel. 01473 626618

WI Country Markets Ltd
Tel. 0118 9394646
web: www.wimarkets.co.uk

Woodbridge Museum
Tel. 01394 380502

Akenfield Garden
(Peggy Cole)
Tel. 01473 737402

Easton Farm Park
Tel. 01728 746475
Fax. 01728 747861
web:
www.eastonfarmpark.co.uk

visitors, who can buy special food pellets from the entrance kiosk.

Children can get even closer to the animals in the pets' paddock which is stocked with many of the tamer animals from the park.

During the Spring and early Summer there are regularly a number of new arrivals, such as piglets.

The park's other facilities include a gift shop, pony rides, a picnic site and tearoom as well as a number of walks.

Easton is open daily (except Mondays other than in July and August or Bank Holidays) between 10.30am and 6pm from mid-March to the end of September.

Newbourne Springs

Newbourne, eight kilometres (five miles) from Woodbridge, is owned by Anglian Water but managed by volunteers from Suffolk Wildlife Trust (Tel. 01473 890089; Fax. 01473 890165).

For some 50 years – from the 1930s until the early 1980s – it was the main water source for the surrounding district.

There is a circular walk of between one and two hours around the 16.5-hectare (41-acre) reserve, which features a massive variety of habitats.

Otley Hall

An outstanding 15th century moated hall set in four hectares (ten acres) of gardens and boasting links with America and Shakespeare.

The gardens are open between 2pm and 5pm from mid-April to mid-September and the hall is open as well between 12.30pm and 6pm on

Sutton Hoo

certain week-ends in April, May and August (phone for details).

Rendlesham Forest

This 3035 hectare (7500 acre) production forest, with pines and between 20 and 30 other tree varieties including beech, birch, cherry, maple, oak, poplar and sycamore, is eight kilometres (five miles) outside Woodbridge.

There are walks and cycle trails (cycle hire available) through the range of habitats, which includes heath and pond areas.

In 1987 half the forest – half a million tons of timber – blew down overnight in a hurricane but it is gradually recovering.

Among the more curious things for which Rendlesham is known is a UFO sighting at Christmas in 1980.

Special activities are held throughout the year and range from fungal forays to nightjar and nightingale walks, an opportunity to interact with birds of prey and Summer holiday activities for children.

Sutton Hoo

The instinctive feeling of an elderly local resident that the place had been inhabited by Saxon warriors led to the discovery in 1939, at Sutton Hoo, near Woodbridge, of the oldest royal burial site in Britain.

The burial at Sutton Hoo is thought to be that of Raedwald, who was chief of all the kings who ruled the south of England from AD599 to 625 and was the head of the Scandinavian dynasty known as the Wuffingas.

But the King's grave is not the only one at Sutton Hoo. There is extraordinary evidence of others who met a very different and somewhat grim end.

They include a

Camargue horses from Valley Farm, Wickham Market

man who was clearly put to a violent death and a ploughman mysteriously buried with his plough.

The treasure is now in the British Museum but there are exhibits connected with the find at Woodbridge and Ipswich museums as well as at the site.

Sutton Hoo is open on Saturdays, Sundays and Bank Holidays from Easter to October and there are guided tours by the Sutton Hoo Society at 2pm and 3pm.

Pre-booked parties are welcome throughout the year.

Valley Farm Riding & Driving Centre

Valley Farm, at Wickham Market, houses a busy riding centre and Camargue stud, as well as offering coaching in skills such as show jumping and stunt riding.

The centre has exclusively white animals, including Britain's only herd of Carmargues.

The famous white horses from the Rhone Delta are renowned throughout France for their strength and versatility and have a calm, unflappable nature.

Other white animals on the farm are Baa Baa the sheep, Billy & Gruff the goats, Muffin the mule, Midget the toy horse, Teasel the long-tailed Jack Russell, Polo the long-tailed white Boxer and white cats Smartie, Sugar, Spice & Bijou.

The white animal collection is open to the public all year round (except Christmas Day) from 10am to 4pm. Entry is free but donations to the centre's charities of the year are welcomed.

Bruisyard Vineyard, Winery & Herb Centre

Here, at this four-hectare (10-acre) vineyard near Saxmundham, visitors can take an audio-guided tour of the vineyard and winery and taste three of Bruisyard's award-winning range of English wines.

The site also includes one of the largest ornamental herb gardens in East Anglia, a sheltered water garden, children's play area, picnic area, restaurant and teashop.

It is open between 10.30am and 5.30pm daily (except Christmas to January 15th).

Framlingham Castle

The 900-year-old castle, once the home of the Earls and Dukes of Norfolk, is steeped in history.

Originally a power base for the Bigod dynasty, Framlingham was built with a curtain wall with 13 towers – and each tower could be defended by those on either side.

Framlingham also has links with Queen Mary – for it was here that she waited to discover whether she or Lady Jane Grey had been declared Queen after the death of Edward VI.

The 12th century castle, now maintained by English Heritage, has been used as everything from a military fortress to an Elizabethan prison, a poorhouse and a school.

Framlingham is open daily throughout the year from at least 10am and 4pm (10am–6pm from the beginning of April to the end of September) all year round.

A free interactive audio tour is available, along with a children's activity book, and on site there is parking, a museum of domestic bygones and farm tools (open daily between 11am and 1.30pm and 2pm and 4.30pm from Easter to September), shop and toilets with disabled facilities.

Long Shop Steam Museum

A chance to discover the unique history of the village of Leiston at the place where the original Garrett steam engines were made.

This award-winning museum is open between 10am and 5pm from Monday to Saturday and 11am to 5pm on Sundays from the beginning of April to the end of October.

Saxtead Green Post Mill

Maintained by English Heritage, this corn mill just north of Framlingham, is full of mill machinery and the superstructure still turns to face the direction of wind.

The mill is open between 10am and 6pm (closed 1–2pm) from the beginning of April to the end of September and between 10am and 5pm in October with a free audio tour available.

Shawsgate Vineyard

A six hectare (15-acre) vineyard, which was established in 1973 and has undergone major restoration.

Awards won by wines from Shawsgate, which is close to Framlingham, include the gold medal and trophy for the outstanding English wine in 1990 and 1994.

The vineyard, which has a children's play area, picnic area and shop, is open seven days a week between 10.30am and 5pm in Summer (check for Winter opening times).

Group visits can be arranged by appointment.

Otley Hall
Tel. 01473 890264
Fax. 01473 890803

Rendlesham Forest
Tel. 01394 450164
Fax. 01394 450197

Sutton Hoo
Tel. 01394 411288
e-mail: visits@suttonhoo.org

Valley Farm
Tel. 01728 746916
e-mail: sarah@
valleyfarm.demon.co.uk
web: www.valleyfarm.
demon.co.uk

**Bruisyard Vineyard,
Winery & Herb Centre**
Tel. 01728 638281

**Framlingham Castle
(English Heritage)**
Tel. 01728 724189

Long Shop Steam Museum
Tel. 01728 832189

Saxtead Green Post Mill
Tel. 01728 685789

Shawsgate Vineyard
Tel. 01728 724060
Fax. 01728 723232

Framlingham Castle

Index